A PAINTER'S QUEST

ART AS A WAY OF REVELATION
PETER ROGERS

With an Introduction by José Argüelles

1. THE HERMIT   25″ × 24″   1978

BEAR & COMPANY, SANTA FE, NEW MEXICO

Library of Congress Cataloging-in-Publication Data
Rogers, Peter, 1933-
    A painter's quest : art as a way of revelation /
Peter Rogers : with an introduction by José
Argüelles.—2nd ed.
        p.   cm.
    ISBN 0-939680-50-5
        1. Rogers, Peter, 1933-   2. Rogers, Peter,
1933-   —Sources. 3. Painters—United
States—Biography.
    I. Title.
    ND237.R714A2   1988
    759.13—dc19
    [B]   88-12056
                                                                        CIP

Second Edition

Bear & Company
P.O. Drawer 2860
Santa Fe, NM 87504

Design: Angela C. Werneke
Typography: Casa Sin Nombre, Ltd., Santa Fe
Printed in the United States of America
9 8 7 6 5 4 3 2 1

Photography: Ken Cobean, cover, 3, 4a, 4b, 13-19, 36-38, 40, 42, 43, 45, 46, 48-50,
52-55, 63-68, 71-76, 78-81, 82, I-XXVII; A. C. Cooper, 5-10, 21-34, 41, 56-62;
Anthony Vinella, 1, 77, and Santa Fe portrait of artist; Brad Bealmear, 51, XXVIII;
David Hoptman, 2, 35, 69; Lynn Lown, 20; Hazel Jaramillo, 44; S. Rudy, 39.

2. THE PROPOSAL   82″ × 60″   1979

To Jenny, Carol, and Kate with love.

The artist in the doorway of his Santa Fe studio, 1978

CONTENTS

3. THE ENTRANCE TO THE FOREST I   14″ × 13″   1974

FOREWORD

The quest described in this book is what all of us, in our heart of hearts, know should be engaging our full attention during our lives on this planet.

We occasionally "come to ourselves" and realize this. Certain people in each generation, and Peter Rogers is among these, know it always and direct their lives by it.

The age in which we live supports many good painters and sculptors, but most of them have literally nothing to say. On the other hand, there are only too many people with less talent who have plenty to say but no valid means of expressing it.

Peter Rogers is that rare and fortunate being, a first-class painter by any standards who has something to say that is of vital interest to all his generation. Such men have helped the flow of consciousness that combats the apathy and doubts that assail us all. Like Giotto and Blake, he reminds us of our childhood dreams and aspirations.

Others will be inspired by his example. Peter Rogers has lived by his quest and for it, ever since he was a boy.

DAVID WYNNE
LONDON, 1985

INTRODUCTION

Peter Rogers is one of the great visionary artists of the Industrial Age. True to the spiritual and timeless, individual and collective nature of the Quest, the words and images of Peter Rogers are harmonic complements to each other. Indeed, so completely interwoven are the artist's thoughts and paintings that *A Painter's Quest* should be regarded as a visionary gospel intended to incite a moral and uplifting awareness for this time of ultimate peril and opportunity.

Almost everyone who picks up this book will find the title intriguing, while the name of the author will draw the proverbial blank. Who is Peter Rogers? Not that the answer to the question will ultimately add anything to the experience of the paintings and imagery that accompany the text to this highly unusual book. *A Painter's Quest* is not an autobiography and, indeed, Peter Rogers tells us precious little about himself, other than that he was born and educated in England, has had a number of "visionary" experiences, and makes his living in New Mexico, where he has resided for over twenty years.

Clearly not a household name—a Picasso, a Warhol, a Matisse—what is it that gives Peter Rogers, a virtual artistic unknown, the authority to write about his experience in the context of revelation? The answer is quite simple: genuine fidelity to the creative process as a path of self and universal knowledge.

It is this fidelity that sets Rogers apart from the great number of practicing contemporary artists. In an age marked—flawed, one might add—by the indulgent severity of its materialism, causing most artists, painters anyway, to pursue a style or innovative gimmick whose uniqueness is ranked by its commercial marketability, Rogers' Quest possesses an almost medieval, archetypal tone. Here is an artist whose concerns are genuinely philosophical, religious, mystical, and takes seriously the notion that art, along with science, religion and philosophy, is one of the four ways of knowing and expressing the truth.

With the exception of art critic Roger Fry, Rogers' literary references are drawn more from the realm of myth and the perennial philosophy than from the annals of modern art. Robert Graves, P. D. Ouspensky, Chogyam Trungpa and Heraclitus inform Rogers with values that place him more on a footing with the Knights of the Round Table in pursuit of the Grail than with the scramble for fame in Soho. Indeed, here is an artist heroically willing enough to take on *The Three Lords of Materialism*, a subject matter less obvious but more pervasively threatening than *Guernica*.

Of course, Rogers had first to have gone through twentieth-century art school before the Quest could begin, because in twentieth-century art school no one mentions the Quest. So it was in the mid-1950s, just out of art school, that Rogers' odyssey began. And because Rogers' first concern was the Quest rather than style or fame, his paintings possess their own unique quality. Clearly "twentieth century" with echoes of Picasso and Henry Moore, the paintings will appear anachronistic to those accustomed to the avant-garde, while those less concerned with the vagaries of fashion and style may be more disposed to see in them a startling freshness of vision.

Because Rogers' concern is the communication of insight about enduring human values, his paintings are refreshingly accessible. At the same time, however, they are haunting and often ominously powerful. If Rogers' paintings are reminiscent of the work of other artists, they hearken to the great visionary painters of the Industrial Age—Goya, Blake, Redon. Like these other visionary visualists, Rogers has found it necessary to hew his path in isolation. Outrageously moral in his concern, his individualism, like that of Blake's, Goya's or Redon's, is more a reaction against the warped materialism of the age than any need to separate himself out from his fellow humans. Yet in this isolation, there is a mirror in whose luminous reflection each of us may read the design of our own relation to both the inequities of our age and to the beckoning of the great Unknown.

In the process of his Quest, Rogers' innocence is touching. His visionary experience in the concert hall leading to a series of paintings of the life of Christ, which when exhibited in the 1960s, drew upon himself the bored wrath of the critics, is most telling. On the one hand, Rogers plunged ahead ingenuously after the concert hall vision, thinking it had to do with the Ascension of the historical Christ. Following the exhibit and the response of the critics, Rogers does not castigate his critics, but looks even more deeply into himself, and into the nature of the Christ. What he discovers in what he thought was the image of the Ascension is *The Channel*, "the opening of consciousness to the Source, so that individual consciousness may become a channel (the column of light) for the Light of the Source (Reality) to manifest in the world. As such, I saw it to be *the* goal of our existence here on Earth—the only possible next step up the evolutionary ladder."

Rogers' moral and visionary commitment make him truly an *artiste engagé*, the kind of artist that the great existential philosophers Camus or Sartre would have applauded. Yet, there is in A *Painter's Quest*, a simplicity and a harmony that place Rogers and his work in the middle of that mystic circle of those who are elite by virtue of their capacity to dwell in the innocent and timeless power of love.

I think more than anything else it is the innocence of Rogers' Quest that communicates, that makes it familiar, that causes one to stop and return to oneself in recognition of the fact that the Quest is universal, the pattern of life itself. That Rogers is able to show us how the clues to the unfolding of the universal pattern arose from his own search and the details of his own life is most instructive. If a new paradigm, or vision, of wholeness and harmony is to take root, it can only do so through each one of us taking responsibility for the Whole as it manifests in the everyday details of our individual lives.

So it is that A *Painter's Quest* is exemplary. It is a model of this new vision, a complete expression of the hidden harmony which is the world itself. Being such a model or example, A *Painter's Quest* goes a long way toward restoring art to its principle place in the purification and renewal of the world.

May all beings take heart in this visionary gospel that it may illumine the way through the great crisis and moral confusion that mark this time of ultimate opportunity.

JOSÉ ARGÜELLES, PH.D.
BOULDER, COLORADO
DECEMBER 1986

ACKNOWLEDGEMENTS

To begin with, I want to thank all those patient friends who have read my manuscript at various stages and have given me much good advice and valuable criticism: Jack Good, David Wynne, Bill Kirschke, Kate Krasin, Lilian Arias, and especially Michael Mott who, in the throes of writing a book of his own and a busy teaching schedule, took the time to write a detailed critique eight pages long. My thanks also to Jenny, Carol, and Kate, who in their different ways have given me the confidence and inspiration to pursue my goals as an artist; to Joel Goldsmith whose teaching opened my eyes and set my feet firmly on the path; to Jane Clarke for encouraging me to write; to my art teacher at Sherborne, Mrs. Gervis, for encouraging me to paint, and to Vivian Pitchforth and Andrew Freeth for teaching me to draw; to Bill and Melissa, and David and Gillian for their faithful friendship through good times and bad; to my mother and father, and my parents-in-law, Peter and Henriette Wyeth Hurd, for their long-standing love and support; to Cecil Collins and Kathleen Raine for their encouragement at a time when it was badly needed; to Thetis Blacker and Elizabeth Stevenson for their enthusiasm and practical help; to all my patrons too numerous to mention, but especially to Robert O. Anderson, Tug Wilson and Michael Zakroff; to my editors, Gerry and Barbara Clow, without whose vision this book would never have seen the light of day; and finally heartfelt thanks to those friends and patrons whose generosity has made it possible to produce *A Painter's Quest* in color: Frank and Geraldine Hackett-Jones, Gale and Didi Freeman, and John and Barbara Bauchman.

PREFACE

I am a painter. This book is about my painting and is full of pictures, so in an obvious sense this is an art book. It is also an autobiography of sorts since much of it concerns my life, but it is neither a conventional autobiography nor a conventional art book. Stated simply, this book is about a quest and the part played in that quest by my painting.

The quest I am speaking of is a quest for knowledge—"Art is a definite way of knowledge."[1] Together with science, religion, and philosophy, art is one of the four ways of the spiritual life of humanity. The knowledge to be acquired is spiritual knowledge. In other words, properly understood, art is a means to enlightenment. It is the purpose of this book to try to justify that statement and in so doing to give the reader some insight into what it means, or can mean, to be an artist.

A quest implies a journey, but the quest for enlightenment is a journey that takes one not only through the world of physical reality and consciousness, but into the world of the unconscious. Art is "a definite way of knowledge" partly because it provides a means of access to this inner world; it bridges the gap between conscious and unconscious.

I was twenty-three when I began my own quest, so it is a journey that so far has spanned thirty years of my life. During that time, by means of all manner of clues and the unraveling of riddles, and often in spite of myself, a coherent theme, or myth, has emerged in and through my painting. This myth, which is itself the story of the perennial quest for enlightenment, I call simply *The Quest*.

The imagery of *The Quest* began to evolve in 1956, which was the year that I left art school, but it was not until 1966 that I became aware of any theme in my work. Since then I have come to realize that the evolution of this theme has been entirely dependent on the extent to which my conscious mind has

4a. THE GIFT II   16″ × 12″   1975

been able to keep pace with the gifts of the unconscious, and in practice I have found my understanding lagging far behind the receipt of these gifts, as will be evident from the stories I have to tell.

That the imagery of *The Quest* series stems from the *collective* unconscious only gradually became apparent to me as I began to run across precedents in the cultures of past ages; there are echoes, not only of Christian myth, but also of Buddhist, ancient Egyptian, ancient Greek, Chinese, and pre-Christian Irish myth. This merely corroborates what many others have discovered: that there is and always has been only one story—one quest for one goal—and that the same story is to be found in some shape or form within the religious records of all races, regardless from where or when they derive. *The Quest* is my own attempt to find new forms to express this timeless myth, the evolution of the theme being partly the result of my own quest and, paradoxically, partly the means to it.

Nowhere in this book will the reader find the story of *The Quest* told in so many words; it would take a poet to do so successfully and I am not a poet. Instead, towards the middle of the book there is a brief pictorial Quest. I make little attempt at annotation. Paintings should speak for themselves, and it would be wrong to suppose that they are meant to say precisely the same thing

14

to everyone—they never do. Even my own interpretation is subject to change, so I have learned better than to state categorically what my paintings mean. Not that I mean to give the impression that my imagery is obscure; it is mostly self-explanatory and, where it is not, ample clues will be found throughout the book.

I divide what I have to say into two parts. Part One concerns my quest for imagery. As an account of personal experience it is unique, but only because no one quest is ever the same as another. Part Two, which is relatively brief, is less personal in character, for it is about the everyday concern of all artists, which is the creative process itself. Over the years, as I questioned its significance, I began to see the creative process as a metaphor of life. Once seen in this light, its implications prove to be not only timeless but timely too.

Science, philosophy, religion and art are the four ways of knowledge, mysticism the common ground between. Together they provide the pool of human knowledge that determines how we perceive reality. Today science is contributing more to the enlightenment of human consciousness than any other way. The work of the visionary physicists and their scientific new paradigm are

4b. MAN, WOMAN, HORSE, AND DOVE   12″ × 10″   1974

15

changing our perception of reality. Parallels have been drawn between their discoveries and the insights of the mystics, thereby enabling us to make cross-references with other ways of knowledge. Such mental and spiritual activity is vital, for only in the common ground of mysticism is the truth discernible. In this book I hope to fashion a comparable synthesis of mysticism and art.

Whereas religion is founded on revelation, art is a *way* of revelation. Revelation is the manifestation of divine truth and it is precisely this that artists court through their craft. They may not think of it in those terms, but it is because of this fact, and this fact alone, that art may be seen as a legitimate way of knowledge. Not that I care for the word "knowledge"—it is too cold, too cerebral a word. Artists create from the heart, not the head; one speaks of their vision, not their knowledge, and vision goes hand in hand with revelation. This book is an account of my own revelations. So purposeful have they been in their gradual unfolding, so universal in their implications, that I find it hard to believe that they were meant only for me. The story *demanded* to be told, the paintings being the warp woven into the woof of the plot. After thirty years, the parts have come together to form a coherent whole, but the story is far from finished. Rather it is ever changing, ever evolving, for the Quest is a journey that has no end.

PETER ROGERS
SAN PATRICIO, NEW MEXICO
DECEMBER 1986

Note: In the light of those last words, it should be no surprise that, since the publication of the first edition of A Painter's Quest, *I have come to see certain things more clearly. For this second edition I have made some minor additions to the ends of Chapters Six and Seven and some rather more substantial additions to the central section of Chapter Eight.*

PART ONE

5. Man Crossing a Bridge   7″ × 12″   1949

ONE

FOUNDATIONS

When I was sixteen, which was in 1949, I made a pen-and-ink drawing of a man in a hat and macintosh crossing a rickety wooden footbridge over a narrow gorge (5). Beneath him a cataract swirls and splashes, spilling into a lake far below. A strong wind is blowing, perhaps presaging a storm. The path he is following ascends steeply on the other side of the bridge and disappears over the top of a rise, but it runs dangerously near the edge of a cliff. Where he has come from there is a fence around the cliff; where he is going, there is none.

In certain respects the drawing is reminiscent of the Tarot card of the Fool. The Fool, carefree and head in air, is oblivious of the precipice at his feet, and the man in my drawing, although he is hardly carefree, is blind to what lies ahead too. The hat he holds onto with one hand, as he bends with the wind, obscures his vision, but fortunately he, like the Fool, has a small dog trotting at his heels. In many myths animals play the part of guardian spirits. For instance, in the *Mahabharata*, Prince Arjuna's little dog that follows him so faithfully throughout all his adventures turns out to be Brahma Himself. I had no such thoughts when I made the drawing—the dog was just a dog—but I know more now and am glad I put him in. Implicit in the drawing is the question: Where does this dangerous path go?

Within seven years of making this drawing I was to be on such a path myself. Of the intervening years there is little to say. Having completed my schooling and done my National Service, I enrolled at St. Martin's School of Art in London. My chief concern at this time was how I was to survive as a painter. This was an urgent concern as I had no income other than what I

19

could make from my painting, and I was in love and wanted to get married. Although I paid lip service to a sentimental brand of Christianity, in fact I was as materialistic as most people. Whatever genuine spiritual life I had enjoyed as a child had long since been dinned out of me by school and army. Spiritually, I was asleep. However, when I was twenty-three something happened to wake me up—something that would profoundly affect the course of my life.

During the summer vacation in 1956 I made a trip to Monaco, where my fiancée of two years' standing was dancing with a ballet company. One night I was alone in my room in the small pension where I was staying, writing two letters—one to my parents and the other to my future parents-in-law. I was trying to find words to justify our getting married (which was far from easy, since I was still an art student and had scarcely any money), when I heard some words spoken softly and deliberately in my ear. They were, "Seek first the kingdom of heaven within, and the rest shall be added unto you," which, as it turned out, was a garbled version of Luke 12, verse 31. I had only the vaguest notion as to what was meant by "the kingdom of heaven within," but I determined to seek it whatever it was. After all, I had never "heard voices" before and the words seemed to me so timely and to the point that I could hardly ignore them. My quest began that night.

THE PROBLEM OF EVIL

Since the discovery of the Nag Hammadi manuscripts in Egypt in 1945, there has been a new resurgence of interest in the Gnostics. These people, who lived in Egypt in the second and third centuries A.D., were Christian mystics. They refused to have anything to do with the Church hierarchy, which they considered stood in the way of their private quest for enlightenment, and they deplored martyrdom, considering such self-sacrifice misguided. They would also undoubtedly have deplored the Crusades, but by then they had ceased to exist as a recognizable group.

I was surprised to discover recently, although perhaps I shouldn't have been, that initially my quest followed much the same pattern mapped out by the Gnostics 1800 years ago. The Gnostics apparently believed that the process of self-discovery begins as people experience the anguish of the human condition, as they experience confusion, or what was called "aporia," which literally translated means "roadlessness." In her book on the Gnostics, Elaine Pagels says that "Gnostics came to the conclusion that the only way out of suffering was to realize the truth about humanity's place and destiny in the universe. Convinced that the only answers were to be found within, the Gnostic engaged on an intensely private interior journey."[2]

In 1956, while many people were expressing their righteous indignation over the almost bloodless seizure of Suez by Anglo/French troops, there were many more, myself included, who were far more shocked by the tragic fate of the Hungarians. I was at that age when one is particularly sensitive to the wrongs of the world, and the Hungarian Revolution and its aftermath crystallized those feelings. As a painter, I wanted to make some statement about it,

6. THE CRUCIFIXION   70″ × 120″   1957

but the more I considered the problem, the more puzzled I became as to what form to give such a statement. I had no wish to try to emulate Picasso's *Guernica*, nor did I see myself as a political painter in the tradition of the Mexican muralists. At the time, we were living in Monaco, having been married in October in London, and while my wife was dancing I (most improbably in that playground of casinos and nightclubs) was painting a large Crucifixion (6). It had been inspired by my first sight of photographs of the Turin Shroud. For the time being, therefore, the problem was left in abeyance, but that did not mean it left my mind.

7.   8.   9.

In 1958, back in London, I returned to the problem, but it seemed as insoluble as ever and, unable to come up with the means of venting my sense of outrage at the wrongs of the world and at a loss for any more challenging project, I began painting imaginary figures—first one, then two, then three—using earth colors for the most part, and with no ideas other than those of composition and the proper use of paint (7, 8, and 9). Sometimes the figures were seated and sometimes standing. Usually they were female. I did not know where this would lead me, but the pictures were to prove the simple start of a major undertaking. In a sense they were the beginning of the *Quest* series, and

10. An Image of Evil   30″ × 40″   1959

as such the series began in terms of form rather than content. Meaning was now to be breathed into these forms to make them live, this marriage of form and content being the result of my continuing concern with the problem of evil.

Pagels says that "When Gnostic Christians inquired about the origin of evil they did not interpret the term, as we do, primarily in terms of moral evil. The Greek term 'kakia' (like the English term 'ill-ness') originally meant 'what is bad'—what one desires to avoid, such as physical pain, sickness, suffering, misfortune, every kind of harm."[3] Although in those days I had never heard of the Gnostics, it was in this sense that I, too, understood evil. I realized the futility of pointing an accusing finger at, for instance, the Mongol troops who had been brought in to crush the Hungarians. They may have been the instru-

23

ment of evil, but they were under orders and, to all intents and purposes, had no choice in the matter. However, the fact that evil was not primarily a question of morality did nothing to account for its existence.

In an effort to come to grips with the problem, and at a loss for a better solution, I returned to my Crucifixion composition. Extracting the huddled group of three soldiers casting lots for Christ's robe and removing them altogether from that context, I painted them more in the manner of the small figure compositions I had just been working on. The resulting image certainly evoked evil (10). Since I painted little else for the space of a year, there were those who began to doubt my sanity, but I was hoping that, through sheer perseverance, I would come to an understanding of the object of my obsession, but no such understanding occurred.

Eventually, becoming disgusted and depressed by the negativity of what I was painting, I began to search in my mind for a positive image. I wanted to paint the very opposite, but what was the opposite of an image of evil? The obvious answer was an image of good, but where does one draw the line between "the Good" and goody-goodiness? Goody-goodiness is not only objectionable, it is also inherently weak, and I wanted the positive image to be every bit as strong, or stronger, than the negative. I did not know how to paint an image of good. Perhaps the opposite of an image of evil was not so much an image of good as of God, but how does one paint God? I had reached an impasse.

ONENESS AND SEPARATENESS

That summer my wife was performing with a company at the Edinburgh Festival and I went up there with her, but in spite of all the feverish creative activity, my mind was largely occupied with the contents of a book I had just been reading. It was my introduction to mysticism, and at first I found the contents strange, even shocking, but the more I read, the more interested I became. It was an early work by Krishnamurti. In it he talked about humanity's apparent separation from God, which he said was illusory, for we are all in essence divine beings; and he went on to explain that there can only be one goal for

11. THE ILLUSION OF SEPARATENESS   36″ × 48″   1960

12. THE UNDERSTANDING OF ONENESS   36″ × 48″   1960

the mystic, which is the attainment of conscious union with God. At the time, I made no connection between what I was reading and the problem I confronted in my painting.

Since I had to leave before the end of the Festival, I returned to London alone. I traveled by night, but even so the train was crowded and I found myself standing in the corridor. I was watching the dark landscape go by, not thinking of anything in particular, when I heard two phrases spoken with great clarity: "The illusion of separateness" and "The understanding of oneness." It took me a moment to get the point. Then I realized that this was the solution I had been looking for—that I had found the answer to the riddle, "What is the reverse of an image of evil?" The answer had depended on finding the clue to the nature of evil itself. I now had that clue and knew for the first time not only what I had been painting, but what I had to paint. Evil was the result of a belief in a state of separateness from God; so if this separation was illusory, the power of evil had to be illusory too. Since I now knew that my *Image of Evil* would be more properly called *The Illusion of Separateness*, it followed that the reverse of *An Image of Evil* was not, as I had suspected, *An Image of Good*, but *The Understanding of Oneness*. I arrived back in London in a high state of excitement.

Soon after my return I painted a new version of *An Image of Evil*, but now, as *The Illusion of Separateness*, it was no longer suggestive of an evil power; rather was it suggestive of ignorance and fear (11). Then I began trying to resolve the image of oneness. I wanted to make it as much the reverse of the separateness image as possible, so I made the figures outward instead of inward facing, and female instead of male (12). I was concerned that this seemed arbitrary but could find no better solution and, in fact, had I had my wits about me, my concern would have been short-lived because the validation of the image was not long in coming.

It was about this time that I happened on the fact that the original Muses of Greek myth—three in number as opposed to the later nine—were Meditation, Memory, and Song.[4] Now, by an odd coincidence, my new image of oneness seemed to illustrate this concept of the Muses exactly. Instead of recognizing this as the validation it was, though, I was disconcerted because, at the time, the Muses seemed to me irrelevant to the concept of oneness. So it was that I quickly became disenchanted with the new image. It was certainly strange that I had accidentally painted the Muses, but I dismissed the episode as an aberration of the unconscious and left it at that. It was to be many years before I realized that it had been no accident at all.

In 1963 I moved to the United States, and 1966 found me living in New Mexico. By that time I had developed a considerable repertoire of imagery, but I was still unaware of any theme in my work until one day I realized that if I placed the various images in a certain order they made a story. It was this discovery that prompted my first self-conscious attempt to produce a series of

13. THE GIANTS I   12″ × 11″   1972

14. THE ILLUSION OF THE GIANTS I   16″ × 12″   1975

paintings depicting the steps and stages in the quest for enlightenment.

The concepts of oneness and separateness were key images in this new series, the image of separateness remaining much the same as I had painted it in London, except that the huddled group of men became giants, sometimes real (13) and sometimes transparent (14) depending on human sensibility. On the other hand, I now based the image of oneness on one of the small groups of three standing women that I had first painted in 1958. This was because, for reasons already stated, I had become disenchanted with my original oneness image. Although my new image succeeded in not suggesting the Muses, however, it failed to suggest oneness. To compound my blundering, finding no rational justification for making the oneness image all female, I tried introducing a male figure into the group. It didn't feel right, and indeed it wasn't.

29

THE LORDS AND MUSES

It was in 1979 that I discovered the Three Lords of Materialism.[5] This Tibetan Buddhist image rang bells in my head, for the Three Lords are Mind, Speech, and Form. I remembered the image I had discarded in 1960 and the fact that the Three Muses had been Meditation, Memory, and Song, and the more I considered these two images in juxtaposition—the ancient Greek and the Buddhist—the more excited I became. I realized that, taken together, they symbolize, on the one hand, the actual machinery that maintains and sustains the illusion of separateness and, on the other, the means whereby we may cut through the illusion and so perceive Reality. The three men of the separateness image were now for the first time individually identified, and it at last dawned on me that the three women of oneness had been identified all along, that meditation, memory, and song symbolize the process of enlightenment itself, meditation being the means by which we come to the understanding of oneness.

Whereas meditation leads to the memory of the true nature of our being, which in turn leads to song or celebration, the mechanics of the illusion seem to work like this: mind, reacting to form, judges good or bad, but when it does so, mind fails to realize that it is mind itself, steeped in concepts of duality, that created those forms in the first place. Our beliefs and fears, crystallized into speech, become still further crystallized in form. Mind then reacts again to the forms so created, and so on in a vicious circle, validating over and over again what we choose to call "reality."

It is evident that this circle of mind, speech, and form can never be broken, but it can certainly be transformed, this transformation being brought about by the activity of the Muses. There has to be a marriage between the Lords and the Muses, and this marriage is what Christian mystics call "The Marriage of Heaven and Earth." When this marriage takes place, the result is predictable: meditation alters the very nature of mind, which alters the substance of speech, and when mind and speech are so transformed, the forms of our experience are also transformed. It was not until 1983 that I evolved an image to depict this marriage in terms of the Lords and Muses, but before I describe how it came about there are a few more points I want to make.

15. THE THREE LORDS OF MATERIALISM I   64″ × 80″   1980

16. THE THREE MUSES   68″ × 80″   1980

The Lords and Muses are aspects of consciousness and, in so far as consciousness creates our reality, the Lords and Muses may be thought of as gods and goddesses. Unfortunately, in the West, we have come to rely almost entirely on the Three Lords—in other words, reason and the phenomenal world—to solve our problems and provide answers. However, without a balance between reason and intuition, without a consideration of the noumenal as well as the phenomenal world, we inevitably lack vision, and this has been the state of affairs, roughly speaking, since the days of Aristotle.

It seems to me no coincidence that the concept of the Three Muses was lost around the third century before Christ, since Western man had embarked on a super "head trip." According to the myth, Mnemosyne, or Memory—in other words, the Hag*—perhaps in revenge or spite, married Zeus and gave birth to the Nine Muses. These nonentities were put under the auspices of Apollo, god of science, suggesting that Western man, to all intents and purposes, was losing his intuitive faculties. The Three Muses were subdivided, categorized, and reduced to another of Aristotle's boring lists, as though, by naming each branch of the arts, the phenomenon of the creative process could be explained. But the role of the original Muses carried far beyond the confines of what we call "art." The concept of the original Muses must have been conceived at a time when life itself was thought of as *the* creative process.

The marriage of Zeus and Mnemosyne was a travesty of the marriage of Heaven and Earth, and the nine Muses a travesty of the original three. The real marriage of Heaven and Earth is that between Zeus and Aphrodite or, in the Christ myth, that between the Holy Spirit and the Virgin Mary; the outcome of the first union being the birth of Eros, and of the second, Christ, both in their respective ways being messengers of love. The Romans, who vulgarized Greek art, also vulgarized Greek myth and, by the time of Christ's birth, had degraded Eros to the fat baby, Cupid. It seems to have been Jesus' mission to penetrate that violent and materialistic world of the Roman Empire to clarify the myth by actually living it, thus demonstrating once and for all the activity of the Christ as it manifests in and through human consciousness. The nativity

---

See Chapter 3, section entitled "The Marriage of Heaven and Earth," p. 61

of Christ consciousness is the phenomenon that enables the creative process, in its broadest sense, to work properly. It is the outcome of the marriage of the third Lord and the third Muse, of form and song.

When the Maiden (song) gives birth to Christ consciousness, she assumes the role of Mother (meditation)*. Meditation initiates the metamorphosis of the Three Lords of materialism, resulting eventually in the total transformation of form. What this implies is that human reality has now been replaced by divine Reality and, when mystics perceive this Reality, I suspect that what they actually perceive is the fact that God is all there is. When God is all there is, it follows that mind is experienced purely as the mind of God the Father; speech as the word (Logos) of Christ the Son; and all form as Spirit manifest. In other words, mind, speech, and form, *in Reality*, are synonymous with the Holy Trinity. If this deduction is correct, the attainment of oneness with God implies the final metamorphosis of the Three Lords.

I should remind the reader that the image of the Three Lords evolved from *The Illusion of Separateness*, and that *The Illusion of Separateness* evolved from the three figures at the foot of the cross in my 1956 *Crucifixion*. It is a long journey indeed from the soldiers casting lots for Christ's robe, but the implication seems to be that, from the start, hidden within those huddled forms had been the full majesty of the Godhead awaiting recognition.

THE NEW PARADIGM

The fact that many young people nowadays view the world with horror and disgust is nothing new, but perhaps they have more reason for doing so today than ever before. No one, least of all the young, can be blamed for believing that the world must be in the grip of some evil force. Nor, when confronted by all the suffering in the world, can they be blamed for arguing that an almighty God cannot also be good—either God is evil, or God must be dead. For some, such beliefs and suppositions persist throughout life.

The evolution of the group of three men that had begun in my work in 1956 had been both meaningful and, on an unconscious level, highly purpose-

---

See Chapter 3, section entitled "The Marriage of Heaven and Earth," p. 61

ful. Their dark beginnings had reflected my own outlook at the age of twenty-three, but with the passing of a further twenty-three years they had, as Mind, Speech, and Form, become neutral—something no longer to be feared. Nevertheless, as the Three Lords of *Materialism* they still symbolized something negative, for the first Lord—Mind—symbolizes the group consciousness of the race, or universal mind, and universal mind is steeped in materialism. Since mind creates our reality, and since our reality leaves much to be desired, one might say that it is high time we changed our mind.

So the problem now was to find the forms to depict the further evolution of human consciousness, how to depict the metamorphosis of the Three Lords.

17. NEW PARADIGM I   120″ × 102″   1983

My initial attempts to make them simply look more enlightened all failed; it seemed an inadequate solution anyway. Since I was aware that the evolution of the Three Lords is dependent on the activity of the Three Muses—that mind can only become enlightened through meditation—the real solution should have been obvious, but four more years went by before I came to it.

In 1983 I went to England, and while I was there, was invited to speak at the Centre for Spiritual and Psychological Studies. I showed slides of my work and spoke about the creative process and also about the evolution of the images of the Lords and Muses. One of the other speakers was a mathematical physicist by the name of Glen Schaefer. During my talk I saw him nodding vigorously and smiling to me from the back of the room. Afterwards he came up and asked me if I was aware that what I had been saying "paralleled the latest thinking in physics." I have long believed that truth can best be found by an approach through as many disciplines as possible, and what Professor Schaefer had to say excited me. So a few days later, in order to continue our conversation, I caught a train to Cranfield, where Professor Schaefer heads the Ecological Physics Group at the Cranfield Institute of Technology. In the course of the evening he talked about the "new paradigm," a term coined by scientists to describe the new framework of ideas and assumptions that is emerging in the world of science—a framework made necessary by the fact that scientists are discovering that they can no longer leave an ordering intelligence, or God, out of their equations. The new paradigm requires more than reason and logic; it demands enlightenment as a *modus operandi*, and to attain enlightenment the masculine intellect has to be imbued with feminine intuition, mind with meditation. "You know what you've got to do of course," said Glen Schaefer. "Get the girls and boys together." The solution was so obvious I was ashamed I had not thought of it myself.

Soon after I returned to New Mexico I began work on the first version of *New Paradigm* (17). I was uncertain whether or not the two groups would integrate successfully, but they fell into place as though, from the start, they had been designed to go together—and no doubt they had been.

36

18. NEW PARADIGM II   42″ × 40″   1986

19. FALLEN BRANCH   18″ × 12″   1969

TWO

CHARADE

Before moving to the United States in 1963, I spent a year in Spain. The town I lived in, which was called Mojacar, was so isolated that few tourists had ever found it. Apart from electricity, there were no modern amenities. The only source of water was a spring at the foot of the mountain and all the water for the town was brought up in pots, either by donkeys or on women's heads. Many of the women still veiled their faces by holding one edge of their headcloth in their teeth.

During much of the year I spent in Mojacar I lived alone and, as might have been expected under such circumstances, I found myself becoming more aware of nature. What was unexpected was that nature seemed to respond to this awareness. On my walks in the mountains, or along the seashore, I would sometimes encounter natural phenomena that, by reason of the sequence in which they came to my attention, seemed to convey meaning. It was as though, defying reason, nature and I were playing a game of charades together; nature acted the clues and I tried to understand them. I shall describe one of these "charades" because it underlines the urgency of the evolutionary process I have just sketched out. It was certainly graphic enough to give impetus to my own quest, even though a complete understanding of it only came much later. This "charade" also demonstrates the fact that the archetypes manifest themselves not only in dreams, but also in waking experience, and sometimes in the most unexpected ways.

One day an American college student who was staying with me borrowed my scooter to explore the coast to the south. He returned with an odd story. He said that if you followed the dirt road along the coast far enough, it ran into a riverbed and, if you followed it inland up the riverbed, it eventually turned south again, becoming a paved highway. The story made no sense. Why would a paved road start in a riverbed and go, so far as I could gather from the map, nowhere? Some weeks later I decided to retrace the route my friend had taken and to continue on the road until I found out where it went, and why.

The sun was high in the sky and it was very hot as I drove down the coast. That part of the Costa del Sol was then quite undeveloped; there were no houses and no people. I had the Mediterranean to my left and the austere range of the Sierra Cabrera to my right and, when I came to the riverbed, I had no choice but to follow it, since further on the mountains dropped straight to the sea. The valley I found myself in was narrow, devoid of vegetation, and enclosed by steep shale hills; the river could not have run for centuries. After about two miles I came to the paved road—it was just as my friend had said—and I followed it up into the mountains, thinking all the while that I was going inland, so that the view when I arrived at the top took me by surprise. A big bay swung in an arc towards the horizon, and in the middle of this arc was a small town, white against the dark blue sea. I wondered at this, since I could remember no seaport or settlement of any kind marked on the map. Beyond, blurred in the heat haze, the mountains came down to the sea again.

Descending the mountain and approaching the town, I could see no sign of life. Perplexed, I went nearer. Then I saw that the houses were not real houses at all; they were, for the most part, nothing but flimsy shells, crudely made of lath and plaster. Some had already collapsed. Built on sand and lacking foundations, none of them would stand for long. A mosque and fort, though more substantial in construction, were already beginning to crumble away, eroded by wind and rain. And yet, from a distance, the town had fooled me. It was a film set. After exploring the silent streets, I left and drove on down the coast.*

Deciding to go for a swim, I parked the scooter by the side of the road, crossed the beach to the sea, and, having cooled off in the water, walked down the seashore all the way to the far end of the bay. Clambering over the rocks

*As I was later to discover, this was the set built for the Aqaba sequence in Lawrence of Arabia.

of a headland, I found myself in a small cove. Confronting me was a skeleton. It was perfectly preserved, from the elegant beak-shaped skull to all the smoothly interlocking vertebrae. It rose out of the sand like a sea serpent and, for the life of me, I could not make out what it was, although it was certainly beautiful and I studied the bone structure in wonder. On an impulse I began to dig around it, but beneath the sand the body of the animal was still intact though badly decomposed, and, where I had dug, thousands of maggots came swarming out. I left the cove in revulsion.*

I began walking back down the beach but had not gone far when I saw that someone was standing at approximately the place where I had left my belongings. Soon I was able to see that it was a Civil Guard in his tricorn hat, with a rifle slung from his shoulder. He had not seen me and was looking out to sea and down at my scooter and, for all I knew, thinking its owner must have drowned. He was holding something in his hand, although what it was I could not at first make out. Eventually, of course, he saw me. Coming up to him, I quickly explained myself, all strangers being smugglers until proven otherwise. I looked at the object he was holding. Dangling from his fist by its hind legs was a small rabbit, dead, with empty eye sockets; myxomatosis or not, he was taking it home to eat. He explained he had run over it and, convinced I was harmless, mounted his bicycle and peddled off.

Perhaps I had had too much sun; in any event, by the time I got home I was running a fever and thankfully went to bed and to sleep. But I could not have slept for long before a loud bang woke me up again—later I found a lump of cement sticking to a windowpane, flung, presumably, but some local workman—and, in the moment of waking, those images on the beach flashed through my head. It had been exactly like waking from a vivid, if puzzling, dream.

The precise meaning of this charade eluded me for many years. Its eventual interpretation was due to my discovery of the Three Lords of Materialism, but I doubt that I'd have made the connection between the Three Lords and those images on the seashore had it not been for a trip I made in 1980. I had

---

*The skeleton must have been that of a camel used in the film.

been commissioned to paint a mural for an oil company in Mexico and, although I was in a big city, in certain respects the circumstances were reminiscent of my time in Spain. Again I was living alone and unable to communicate intelligently, since in the intervening eighteen years my Spanish, always minimal, had deteriorated rather than improved. I found myself travelling back in memory to Mojacar, to the coast road down which I had driven for no other reason than to find out where it went. As I relived the events of that day, I realized that I now had the key to their meaning.

The valley I had driven through before coming to the paved road had been grim, the steep hills crowding in like slag heaps, the sun reflecting off the black shale making it oppressively hot. There had been no breeze to stir the air, no birds, nor any living thing. By contrast, the air at the top of the mountain had been fresh and the view arcadian. Furthermore, the seaward side of the coastal range was lush with vegetation, and there were birds—a hawk had preceded me down the mountain.

The mountaintop and valley, beauty and ugliness, life and death—the opposites had been extreme and, perhaps because I was alone in a wild and desolate place and consequently more sensitive than usual to nature's moods, my conflicting reactions had been extreme too. Whereas in the valley I had felt a sense of unease verging on dread, on the mountaintop my spirits had been lifted dramatically by the grandeur that confronted me. If, as I believe, I was to be taught something of importance that hot summer day in Spain, then as a necessary prelude I was made to *feel* duality.

"And here is the fruit of duality, the fruit of the Tree of Knowledge of Good and Evil," and the fruit had proved rotten indeed: destruction, decay, and death each confronted me in turn upon the seashore. To begin with, the city had been a fake, the brilliant sunlight having whitewashed the shabby and crumbling reality. Then the skeleton—its structure had been beautiful, but out of it had come maggots and the stink of decay. And then the rabbit in the clutches of a man with a gun—it had been run over by a bicycle, like valley and mountaintop, another symbol of duality. Farfetched? I do not think so, because in dreams everything is symbolic, and the events of that day were more like a dream than a waking experience.

Mind, Speech, and Form, the Three Lords of Materialism, are both the cause and effect of reality as we experience it. They are, thank God, capable of metamorphosis, for, if those images on the beach were, as I believe, metaphors of reality, they suggest that human consciousness (mind) is blind like the rabbit—that we are helpless victims of our own fears and aggressions (the man with a gun); that language (speech), structurally beautiful in and of itself (the skeleton), is so abused that it may indeed be said to be maggot-ridden; and that our civilization (form), superficially brilliant, is in reality a fake (the city).

Mystics tell us that in Reality there is only oneness, so any form that stems from the dualistic nature of human material consciousness must of necessity in ultimate terms be considered fake, or what the Hindus would call *Maya*. But the city was not only fake, it was deserted and in ruins; the rabbit not only blind, but dead. Was this some gruesome prophecy? I hope not. I prefer to think the charade implied that where the road goes is up to us, at the same time spelling out two cold, hard truths: that all civilizations die and crumble away because they are founded in duality and not oneness; and that, like the blind rabbit, all of us will continue to be the seeming victims of forces outside our control until we open our eyes to the truth about who we really are.

At work on ASCENSION mural, Mojacar, 1962

THREE

A VISION

The facts concerning our true identity had already been brought home to me shortly before my trip to Spain in 1962. This personal revelation came about through my painting, but the sequence of events leading up to it began with a vision I had in 1960.

Improbably, the vision took place in the Albert Hall in London. We had been given tickets for a concert. It was a "promenade" concert so the seats had been removed from the floor of the auditorium and people came and went as they pleased. Since this was distracting, I had shut my eyes.

I read somewhere recently that it is not uncommon before a mystical experience to have the sensation, like Alice, that one is growing. This happened to me, although it was not all of me that suddenly began to grow, but just my hands, which were folded in my lap. They were becoming so big that I felt they would soon fill the entire hall. It was at this point, in the middle of a symphony by Cesar Frank, that the girl appeared.

She was coming towards me out of the night. She was quite close to me, looking straight at me, but although she was still moving forward it was as though the ground receded from under her, because she came no closer. Beyond her I could just make out the line of the horizon. Above, where the clouds parted, there were dark blue spaces of unfathomable depth; looking at them gave me a feeling of vertigo, so I switched my attention to a form on my left. At first conscious only of its mass, I presumed it to be a rock until a movement made me aware that in reality it was a group of men and women, all huddled together, gazing up into the sky. Then another figure appeared—a woman kneeling; she too was gazing up, her head thrown back and her arms raised as though in supplication. She was dressed in blue and was right in front of me. From the direction in which the girl had come I could hear waves breaking on a seashore.

Now, when I saw the group of people and the woman in blue all looking up into the sky, I jumped to what may well seem an odd conclusion. I became convinced that what I was seeing was the Ascension, and the fact that I was so certain about this still puzzles me because, since painting the Crucifixion inspired by the Shroud of Turin four years previously, I had lost interest in Christian imagery. When confronted with a bona fide vision, however, it seemed I could not escape my Christian heritage after all; I was confident I was about to see the ascending figure of Christ.

As it turned out, I never did. Instead, I saw something that took me completely by surprise. Out of a vortex of clouds an incandescent ball of fire appeared; it was not a disk—I was very much aware of its volume. It moved in horizontally from the top right, many times bigger than the moon, as bright as the sun, trailing a luminescent tail. (Incidentally, such are the habits of the times that perhaps I should mention I had taken no drug of any sort.)

Now, in a way I cannot fully explain, everything I had seen had been in terms of painting. This is not to say that I could ever hope to recreate in *two* dimensions everything I saw with a heightened sense of awareness in *three*, but throughout the experience one part of my mind was aware of composition, and this I could recreate. I was wondering, for instance, how the vertically ascending figure of Christ was going to work in an otherwise essentially horizontal composition. As an artist, therefore, I was delighted when the ball of fire came in horizontally to complete the design in the most unexpected and dramatic way. I remember thinking that perhaps this was the way Blake saw.

Convinced that what I had seen had been the Ascension, I rationalized the ball of fire as the cloud that "received him out of their sight"; but later, when I began trying to paint what I had seen, I soon realized that the girl who had appeared first in no way fitted the Ascension scenario. I knew that there had been two mysterious "gentlemen in white apparel" present at the Ascension, but the girl, though she had indeed been dressed in white, had certainly not been one of these—she had been the essence of femininity. Furthermore, although I had no explanation for her, I knew that her presence had been important. The trouble was that as soon as I tried to paint her honestly, the picture became "pagan." Eventually I compromised. Knowing it was wrong, but reluctant to give up on my Ascension idea since I had no other, I painted her as an ambiguous male figure who might or might not have been one of the gentlemen in white. Deservedly, the painting was a disappointment, but it was just acceptable as a picture of the Ascension, even if it was the only picture of the Ascension ever painted that included no suggestion of the figure of Christ.

20. THE HERALD   82″ × 66″   1979

THE CHRIST MYTH

For five months in 1960 my wife had been in Italy rehearsing for a ballet festival to be held at Nervi, near Genoa. During that time I had my first one-man show and, on the strength of it, went to Italy myself in time for the first performance. It did not take long for me to realize that all was not well with our marriage, however, and it was partly as a result of the inevitable crisis that ensued and all the unhappiness that went along with it, that something quite unexpected happened—I gained what was, for me, a new insight into the Christ myth.

This unlikely outcome still lay in the future. In the meantime, shortly after our return to London, I began work on a figure composition. It depicted a group of Italian peasants—I had some of Augustus John's compositions in the back of my mind—but, as the picture progressed, the figures became less like peasants and more idealized. In the center of the painting, facing the spectator, stood a woman with a boy and a man with a baby; on the right there was a single man and, facing him on the left, a single woman. I was having difficulty with the composition until I had the idea of raising an arm of the woman on the left. This solved the design problem, but it did more—I realized that unintentionally I had painted an annunciation. The woman was announcing the imminent birth of Christ to the man, whereas the bystanders had already experienced their nativities, the boy and baby being the outward and visible evidence of their evolving Christ consciousness (21).

As I have said, since painting the Crucifixion in 1956 I had lost interest in traditional Christian imagery. I had been trying to evolve new imagery of my own that would cut through the barriers of race and creed and, to some extent, my annunciation painting, in spite of its Christian overtones, belonged in that category. However, because I believed what I had seen in the Albert Hall to have been the Ascension, I found myself considering orthodox imagery again. I resolved to paint a whole series of pictures on the life of Christ, although it was not so much the Ascension itself but rather the way I had seen it that inspired the new series. The vision had been like the gift of a perfect composition and had provided me with a much-needed clue to the direction I should take as a painter. It occurred to me that any event in the life of Christ

48

21. An Annunciation   48″ × 72″   1960

would provide a good excuse to capitalize on this clue.

It was shortly after I had completed the annunciation painting that my marital crisis took a turn for the worse. I was paralyzed with unhappiness and did little but sit in a chair for several days and mope. Eventually, realizing that this was getting me nowhere, I decided to begin the paintings on the life of Christ that I had been intending to start for some time. Since I was solely concerned with relating single figures to groups of figures, such as I had seen in my vision, my choice of subject matter was random. I painted Christ walking on the water with the panic-stricken apostles in the boat in the foreground (22); praying in the Garden of Gethsemane while the apostles slept (23); and raising Lazarus—but since I was unable to make this last composition work, I changed it to an apocryphal incident in which Christ is showing his wounds to the apostles (25). Having completed these three, I painted a Crucifixion triptych (24) and then the descent from the cross (26).

Painting is good therapy, and painting these pictures gave me enough presence of mind to be able to start meditating. In the meantime I continued the series, painting the expulsion of the moneychangers, the Resurrection, and Christ healing the blind, washing the apostles' feet, and teaching Mary. As soon as they were dry I took them to my dealer, and within a few weeks they were all sold.

It was several months later, sometime in the fall of 1961, that the significance of those pictures dawned on me. One morning, while I was washing my brushes in the studio, I had one of those instantaneous realizations that seem to come out of nowhere and for no particular reason. Autobiographical—those pictures had all been about me. As I thought about this, I realized that the key lay in the fact that in every painting my ego had been symbolized by the apostles, whereas the figure of Jesus had symbolized the Christ of my own being. The significance of the paintings became still clearer when I recalled my state of mind at the time I painted them.

I had begun the series when I was feeling sorry for myself. I had been totally involved with my ego, which had been hurt, and was behaving like the apostles in the boat on the stormy sea, crying out because they thought they

22. 31″ × 25″ 1960   23. 36″ × 28″ 1960

24. 60″ × 31″ 1960

25. 32″ × 24″ 1960   26. 31″ × 25″ 1960

27.   30″ × 28″   1961   28.   36″ × 28″   1961

29.   40″ × 30″   1961

30.   20″ × 12″   1961

were sinking. Christ was saying to them, "If you want, you can walk over the stormy water," but, like the apostles in the Garden of Gethsemane, I was asleep to the Christ. Those had been the first two paintings. The third had begun as the raising of Lazarus, and in a sense I too was dead. The Christ of my being wished to raise me from the dead, but I was still denying him—I had destroyed that painting. By denying him I was wounding him, and he showed me his wounds. Since this made no impression, crucifixion was inevitable. Those had been the third and fourth paintings.

It seems to me that the Christ myth demonstrates a choice: we can associate with the Christ of our own being and so receive our inheritance as children of God, or we can associate with our ego, or small sense of self, and suffer the consequences. I was aware of this choice, so I should have known better, but when the crisis came, like Peter in the story, I had denied the Christ. It was at this juncture that I had at last begun to pull myself together, by which I mean I had made a deliberate attempt to identify with my greater sense of self. By making that identification and by relegating the ego to its proper place, the stone had been rolled from the entrance to the tomb and the Christ had been able to resurrect in my experience (29). He had then driven the parasites from my temple (28), healed my blindness, taught me the truth (27), and even washed my feet (30). As a result, I had regained my peace of mind and a difficult situation had been resolved in the best possible way for all concerned. The painted commentary had been thorough and complete.

ASCENSION

It was in the following year that I went to live alone in Mojacar. From the first moment I set foot in the town, I realized the place presented me with an unusual challenge. To live on that mountaintop, with its magnificent views of land, sea, and sky, was to feel almost as though one were in the company of the gods. As an artist, I felt that to justify my living in such a place I would have to paint better than I had ever done before—either that, or the same gods would render me impotent to paint anything at all—and although this may sound fanciful, the feeling was genuine enough. To meet this challenge I resorted to the most powerful experience of my life.

So it was that I spent the first few months in Mojacar painting the Ascension on a fifteen-by-nine-foot wall of my bedroom (page 44). When this was completed, I tackled the same subject on several canvases of different sizes, playing compositional variations on the same theme. Sometimes I included the ascending figure of Christ, and sometimes both "gentlemen in white apparel" (32, 33, and 34). However, I now tried to paint the incandescent sphere as I had actually seen it, and when I painted the enigmatic figure of the girl, I made its luminescent tail describe a halo around her. This was because I felt her to have been in some way connected to that spectacular object—she had been the only person not looking at it, as though for her, and her alone, it was no mystery; but, although I gave her long hair, I was still unable to paint her as I had seen her—she remained an angelic figure of ambiguous sex. I also painted a column of light emanating from the ball of fire and enveloping the kneeling woman. I cannot say that I had seen this column of light, any more than I had seen the halo around the girl, and to this day I do not know what induced me to put it in, except that it helped the composition (31).

The Ascension, although it was the image that had started me on the *Life of Christ* series, had never held much significance for me—I had thought of it as nothing more than the means of Jesus' exit from the physical plane—but as I painted one version after another I began to realize that it signified far more than that. As with the other images in the *Life of Christ* series, I saw it to be highly relevant to individual human consciousness. In fact, one might say that ascension is our ultimate destiny. As in the parable of the prodigal son, it is the return to the father's house, the return, that is, to the state of being that justified Jesus' claim, "I and my Father are one." It implies an opening of consciousness to the Source so that individual consciousness may become a channel (the column of light) for the light of the Source (Reality) to manifest in the world. As such I saw it to be *the* goal of our existence here on Earth—the only possible next step up the evolutionary ladder. When, four years later, in 1966, I began consciously to evolve the *Quest* series, the goal of the quest was, naturally, ascension.

Earlier that year I had come to certain conclusions that gave me an added incentive for starting on such a project. In 1965 I had produced a second series

31. THE ASCENSION I   36″ × 25″   1962

32. THE ASCENSION II   40″ × 50″   1962

of paintings on the life of Christ that was exhibited in London in January 1966. In the course of the show I became painfully aware that, even though the paintings were, for me, charged with meaning that had relevance both to the individual and to the present moment, to everyone else they were merely Bible illustrations. For the most part people reacted with the boredom bred of over-familiarity. The only critic to review the show wrote, "When a young contemporary painter comes out uncompromisingly for Christian subjects we are bound to call him into question." He regarded my work as an anachronism. Clearly, if I was to express the ideas I wanted to express and to communicate those ideas to others, I was going to have to find a new language and new forms. The images of oneness and separateness, the annunciation to the *man*, and the Ascension without Jesus all seemed to be steps in the right direction.

33. THE ASCENSION III   45″ × 60″   1962

34. THE ASCENSION IV   *24″ × 10″*   1963

THE COMET

In 1966 I made a further discovery—one that drastically altered my interpretation of the Albert Hall experience. In fact for several years I quite believed, although wrongly, that the vision had had nothing whatever to do with the Ascension. At the time, it was a healthy belief. For one thing, it forced me out of a mental rut, and for another, it steered me yet further away from overtly Christian imagery. Nor did it disturb me; I found it merely ironic that my mistaken interpretation had led to so much that had been constructive. This new perspective was due to my reading a remarkable book about the history of our planet.

Like many innovative thinkers, Immanuel Velikovsky was much maligned in his lifetime. Even today he is often dismissed as a crackpot, both by those academics who have a vested interest in old ideas and, as a result of their influence, by the media. However, more and more scientists, working in many different fields, are now taking him seriously. In my opinion, few who have read his books can fail to take his remarkable thesis seriously. I accepted it from the moment I read his first book, *Worlds in Collision*, but then I had a special reason for doing so.

The book had been lent to me with no particular fanfare, but by the time I had reached Chapter Three of Part One I was reading with mounting interest. Velikovsky's thesis was this: that within historical times a comet only slightly smaller than Earth had come very near our planet and, due to its magnetic attraction, altered the angle of rotation of the Earth, causing universal devastation; that the Earth passed right through the tail of this comet; that, due to hurricanes, earthquakes, fires, and tidal waves, much of the population of the world perished and several species of animal became extinct; that the comet was eventually tamed into a regular orbit by the Sun, becoming the planet Venus; and that this cataclysmic event was one of several near collisions between Earth and other planetary bodies, Noah's flood having been caused by a previous encounter and the most recent having been with Mars in 687 B.C.

I have no intention of going into the complex ramifications of all the evidence. Suffice it to say that the written evidence alone, apart from the geological and paleontological, is impressive. However, the question arises, why, if these events really happened, do we not know about them? The answer appears to be that people cannot live with the memory of such traumatic events and so have blotted them from memory; but, like all such memories, they remain in the collective unconscious and once in a while come to the surface. I believe that, on one level, that is what happened in the Albert Hall.

Certainly, nothing but a comet has the sort of incandescent tail I saw in my vision. However, it is hardly surprising that I failed to understand what I had seen, my previous experience of comets having consisted of photographs in which they appeared as small streaks of light, whereas the comet in the vision had appeared bigger than the sun. No wonder the people were huddled together—they were terrified; no wonder the woman in blue had her arms raised in supplication—the comet threatened their very existence. Which left the figure of the girl I had seen first, who was not frightened at all, and who seemed completely detached from what was going on. Could she have been the personification of the planet Venus—Venus, the Goddess? (36)

Of course, there is no easy answer to that question. That the vision came from some incomprehensible source within myself and that it stimulated my quest for imagery, are both undoubted facts, but I think it probable that what I saw could only enter my consciousness because, as a traumatic event in the history of the race, it already existed in the collective unconscious. However, the figure of the girl seems to confound the theory that the vision was merely a memory of a traumatic event, and what of the traumatic event itself? Perhaps in some macrocosmic order of things it signified more than our mundane minds can comprehend. In any event I felt that if the girl could be identified, the meaning of the whole would become apparent; but at the time, even

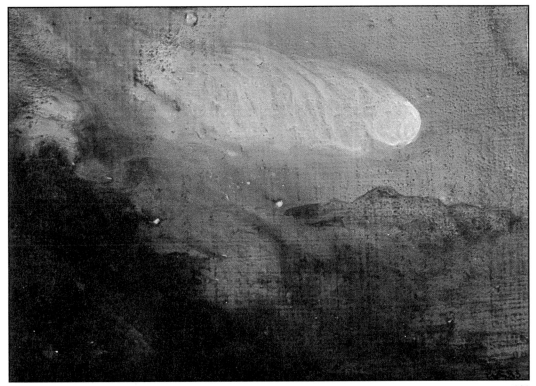

35. THE COMET III   8″ × 6″   1983

36. The Birth of Venus   72″ × 48″   1967

though I was in possession of most of the necessary clues, I failed to understand them. The girl, and hence the vision too, remained a mystery for another fifteen years.

In the meantime, I did at least discover something that threw light on the symbolism of the comet. A neighbor of ours claimed to have seen a flying saucer, and since his excitement stirred my interest, I picked up a copy of Jung's *Flying Saucers* to see what he had to say about them. I am not concerned with his conclusions in this context, but I came on the following statement:

> If the round shining objects that appear in the sky be regarded as visions, we can hardly avoid interpreting them as archetypal images...Anyone with the requisite historical and psychological knowledge knows that circular symbols have played an important role in every age; in our own sphere of culture, for instance, they were not only soul symbols, but "God-images."[6]

It had now been several years since I had first painted the comet, and instinctively I had always thought of it as a divine manifestation. This was the validation I was looking for. I too had seen a round shining object in the sky, and, feeling that Jung's words justified my using the comet as a "God-image," I was able to paint it with confidence as such from then on.

THE MARRIAGE OF HEAVEN AND EARTH

Not many people in our technological civilization are familiar with the Triple Goddess, or White Goddess as she is sometimes called. Industry and concrete jungles are alien to her, and the careless exploitation of the resources of our planet, the pollution of seas and rivers, and the extermination of wildlife constitute her rape—for she is Mother Earth. In the days when people had to live in tune with nature or perish, the Goddess was associated with the seasons: as Maiden she was spring; as Mother, summer; and as Hag, fall/winter. Even after the advent of Christianity her name was honored—the Gnostics, for instance, equating the Goddess with the Virgin Mary, for which heresy they were persecuted—but it was not until the Protestant Reformation in the sixteenth century that an attempt was made to expunge her name entirely.

In medieval times Christian poets identified the Virgin Mary with the Muse, the Muse being their source of inspiration. Robert Graves says that:

> In mediaeval Irish poetry Mary was equally plainly identified with Brigit the Goddess of Poetry: for St. Brigit, the Virgin as Muse, was popularly known as "Mary of the Gael"...in Gaelic Scotland her symbol was the White Swan, and she was known as Bride of the Golden Hair, Bride of the White Hills, Mother of the King of Glory...The mediaeval Brigit shared the Museship with another Mary, "Mary Gipsy" or St. Mary of Egypt... This charming Virgin with the blue robe and pearl necklace was the ancient pagan Sea-goddess Marian in transparent disguise, patroness of poets and lovers and proud mother of the Archer of Love...The Greeks called her Aphrodite...Botticelli's "Birth of Venus" is an exact icon of her cult.[7]

From all this I deduce that the Virgin Mary, who was to become "Mother of the King of Glory," and Aphrodite, or Venus, "proud mother of the Archer of Love," can both be identified with the Muse, and that therefore the Triple Muse and Triple Goddess are one and the same. I would go further and suggest that the Triple Muse and the Triple Goddess equate precisely; that the third Muse, Song, equates to the Maiden; the first Muse, Meditation, to the Mother; and the second Muse, Memory, to the Hag.

No *man* can hope to make progress on the Quest without help from this Muse/Goddess. Symbolizing as she does the feminine, intuitive aspect of the psyche in men, she is vital for balance. She only is perceptive enough to receive the gifts that come to us through the channel of awareness. It is also a fact that

37. HEAD OF A GIRL   14″ × 16″   1972

38. The Return of the Dove I   76" × 66"   1978

38. The woman symbolizes the receptive side of the psyche. She receives the dove (the Spirit of Truth) while the man sleeps. Sometimes the male questing side of the psyche has to be "asleep" for the truth to be discerned. This is why inspiration often comes when least expected (such as when I was standing in the corridor of the night train from Edinburgh).

men project this aspect of themselves onto real women, finding the Muse in their girlfriends and lovers, this outer personification of the Muse being a reflection of an inner yearning for completion, for wholeness, a longing that we often only recognize in dreams or, occasionally, in visions. Which brings me back to the vision in Albert Hall. The theory that the comet became the planet Venus had sown the seed of an idea in my head; perhaps the girl I had seen coming towards me out of the night had been the personification of this Muse/Goddess.

I now believe that the girl was indeed the personification of the Muse—the inner personification. I eventually came to this conclusion as a result of questioning not only what I had actually seen and heard—for I had heard the sound of the sea—but also the way in which I had chosen to paint what I had seen. The girl had been dressed in white, the color symbolic, not only of the White Goddess, but of the bride. The sea, of course, is also a symbol of the Goddess, the name Mary being derived from the same root as the Latin *mare* meaning sea. So, if the girl had been the Goddess, she was the Maiden aspect of the Goddess, the daughter of Mother Earth; and if one accepts the comet as a symbol of the male Godhead then, by painting the tail of the comet encircling the Maiden, I had unwittingly painted an icon of the marriage of Heaven and Earth (39). Since the Virgin Mary and the Muse/Maiden are synonymous, the result of that union with the male Godhead could, in Christian terms, be only one thing—the birth of the Christ in consciousness.

But there is more to the image than that. I have always understood the column of light, such as I painted it in Mojacar, to symbolize the channel of awareness, but recently I realized that this channel of awareness is itself symbolic of the Christ. When Jesus, speaking as the Christ, said, "I of my own self can do nothing—the Father within He doeth the works," he made it abundantly clear that he was the channel for, rather than the initiator of, the works. The Christ *is* the channel. So those Ascensions I painted in Spain were icons not only of the marriage of Heaven and Earth with eventual nativity implied, but of the fruit of nativity, or the activity of the Christ, fully manifest.

This discovery left only one question unanswered: Who was the woman

39. THE MARRIAGE OF HEAVEN AND EARTH   72" × 68"   1981

in blue at the base of the column of light? With her arms upstretched she seemed to be calling down the light of Heaven, or calling the channel into being. As if in answer to the question, I chanced upon the following:

> . . .to live "in the Spirit" is in effect to live in and by Mary, the Bride of the Holy Spirit. Life in the Spirit is a life which she herself has obtained for us and given to us as Mediatrix of all grace. The movements of our life in the Spirit are directed by her motherly heart.[8]

The supplicatory figure of the kneeling woman seems to me a graphic image of this "Mediatrix of all grace," obtaining for us our "life in the Spirit." As such she is another embodiment of the Virgin Mary or Muse/Goddess. This identification is further underlined by the color of her dress, blue being the traditional color of the robe worn not only by the sea-goddess Marian, or Aphrodite, but by Mary the Virgin. I have already identified the girl I had seen first as the bride; the woman in blue could not have been a second personification of this Maiden aspect of the Triple Goddess—for one thing she had appeared to be in early middle age—so the woman in blue must have been the personification of Mary as Mother.

If what I saw in the Albert Hall was indeed the mystical marriage of Heaven and Earth, then such a marriage implies the conception of a new state of consciousness. Following that conception, due to my Christian heritage, I had painted a commentary on the ensuing process in Christian terms. This process is what Christians call "nativity," and, appropriately enough, it had been heralded by an annunciation (21). As with many births, it was a painful process. I had then gone on to paint a commentary on the activity of this consciousness in my own life. Since, at the time, I was ignorant of the true significance of the vision, had it not been for those paintings on the life of Christ, I would have remained completely unaware of what had happened.

There is one final point I want to make. The vision and the image I call *The New Paradigm*, of which I spoke in Chapter One, both express the same idea—both symbolize the marriage of Heaven and Earth. If visually they bear no resemblance to each other, it is simply because *The New Paradigm* evolved from ancient Greek and Buddhist imagery, whereas the vision was couched in

Graeco/Christian terms. *The New Paradigm* evolved as the result of a conscious thinking process, however, the idea coming first and then the image to express the idea, whereas the reverse is true of the vision. The vision was a gift from the unconscious, the meaning of which had then to be unriddled. And yet both images proved to depict the same chain of events. In terms of *The New Paradigm* the union of mind and meditation opens the channel of awareness, which in due course leads to the perception and experience of Reality; in Christian terms, the marriage of Heaven and Earth leads to nativity, which in due course leads to ascension. So it seems that my first impulse to think that what I was seeing was the Ascension was not far from the truth after all.

40. You are looking down from above. Joseph is washing his hands in a bowl of water, having just delivered the baby. He is also symbolically washing his hands of responsibility, for he is not the father. In view of Christ's statement, "Call no man your father upon the earth, for one is your Father which is in heaven," the picture may also be seen as an icon of father-hood in general. Of course, to wash one's hands of responsibility does not mean to imply that one ceases to love one's children and care for their needs. Rather, it implies the recognition that our children are first and foremost the children of God and, as such, in God's hands. Such a recognition is the greatest blessing anyone can bestow on a child, or on anyone else for that matter. "Whom say ye that I am?," asked Jesus of the disciples. Only Peter had the correct answer: "Thou art the Christ, the Son of the living God." In spite of all appearances to the contrary, the same is true of every man, woman, and child on the face of the Earth, and this realization is nativity.

40. THE NATIVITY   40″ × 50″   1961

41. Saint in Meditation   52″ × 60″   1960

FOUR
THE HERMIT

There are times, as a painter, when it seems that nothing will go right; the paint won't flow, and one's painting gets more and more labored, or "tight," to use a painter's expression. I found myself at such an impasse in 1972, and was uncertain how to break it until I remembered a picture I had painted in London in 1960. I had been painting on a large board which I had placed flat on the floor, since I was working wet. I was trying to paint an oriental saint, seated in the lotus position, deep in meditation. I had no trouble stating the figure, but soon ran into problems when I tried to relate him to the surrounding space; nothing seemed to work, and at the end of the day, having made a big mess, I mopped up as much of it as I could and went to bed. In the morning when I returned to the studio, I found the saint sitting on a seashore. Behind him was a storm-tossed sea, while above him the whole firmament swirled in orbit. During the night the puddles of paint I had failed to wipe up had done amazing things. Except for a few flicks here and there to indicate waves, I decided not to touch it; it was far more interesting than anything I could have done intentionally (41).

So it was that there in my New Mexico studio twelve years later, I decided to stop relying so much on my head and to see what happened if I relied more on accident. I had a dozen small birch panels cut and primed and, laying them on the floor, I proceeded to throw paint on them. The channel of awareness was in the back of my mind, and I attacked the little panels as though by sheer violence I could force the channel into being; so to some extent, when I was done, each panel contained a rough vortex of light. Since I was using water-based paints, they were dry enough the following morning to stand on end so

71

42. A VISION OF THE VIRGIN AND CHILD   10″ × 9″   1972

that I could examine what I had done. Some of them, turned horizontally, suggested landscapes; then, in one after another, I began seeing a bearded old man. In some cases he was astonishingly detailed, complete with fingers, facial features, folds in his clothing, and everything in proportion. I had no idea as to his significance, but set about pulling out of the paint whatever it was that appeared to be there, including, in each case, the old man (43 and 45). I decided to call him "the hermit," since he was usually in an otherwise empty landscape. Two pictures were exceptions, for one showed the Virgin and Child appearing to a younger man in a vision, with a whooping crane in the foreground, which

I knew to be sacred to the Goddess (42), while the other depicted the return of the prodigal son.

In due course I incorporated the old man into my *Quest* imagery. The man and woman of the theme, having lost their way in the forest, encounter the hermit, who directs them to a pool into which he tells them to look in order to find out who they really are. When they look in the pool they see the comet, the God-image (XXII and 77). The hermit is their teacher (44). I have returned almost compulsively to the subject of the hermit over the last ten years, but it is only very recently that I have found out why: he is *my* teacher.

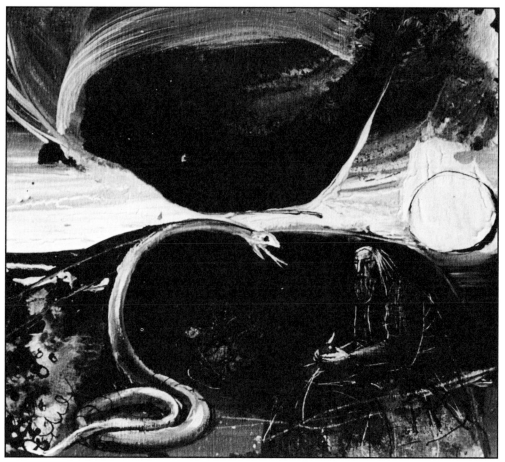

43. HERMIT PEELING AN APPLE   10″ × 9″   1972

This realization came about as a result of reading *The Quest of the Holy Grail*,[9] the second part of the Arthurian trilogy known as "The Matter of Britain." Why, considering my British heritage and the content of my work, I had never read any of the Arthurian legends until this year (1982) I cannot say. Perhaps the Pre-Raphaelites had put me off. In any event, I discovered "The Matter of Britain" to be very much my own.

Of the one hundred and fifty knights that set out from Camelot, only four—Galahad, Percival, Bors, and, to some extent, Lancelot—understood the spiritual nature of their quest. All sought adventures, but the writer makes it clear that the majority returned bewildered and disappointed because not only did nothing much happen to them, but they failed to understand the experiences they did have. Not that Percival, Bors, or Lancelot understood their adventures either at first, but sooner or later they usually encountered a hermit in the forest who would interpret the adventures for them. These sometimes took place in the physical world and sometimes in dreams or visions.

Some of my own adventures have taken many years to fathom, and often the plots have been complex and mystifying. Only gradually have I come to understand their significance, and this, no doubt, is because the hermit is hidden deep in the forest and is hard to find. The hermit is, I believe, the same as Jung's Wise Old Man and therefore is an aspect of one's own psyche. He knows the answers and it seems that, in his own good time, he is prepared to give them. The true identity of this Wise Old Man or archetypal teacher can perhaps be gleaned from what I have already written. The clue is there; in due course I will come to it.

Not long ago I was struck by a curiously simple idea. I imagined myself standing in the dark, holding two short pieces of electrical wire, both of equal length, one in either hand. One symbolized my thoughts and one my feelings. The fact that both were of equal length was important. When I brought the two together, a light came on and I could see.

I am far from being an intellectual, nor have I ever thought of myself as being very perceptive, which is why the two pieces of wire were short—but the fact that they were short did not matter; the light was all that mattered, and,

44. THE TEACHER   11″ × 11″   1975

for the light to manifest, the degree of intelligence or perception was neither here nor there. Intuition might be remarkable, intellect extraordinary, but unless there was a balance between the two, there was no light.

Intellect is considered to be an attribute of the male aspect of the psyche, associated with Heaven, whereas intuition is an attribute of the female aspect of the psyche, associated with Earth, so the marriage of intellect and intuition

75

45. HERMIT WITH SHEEP   9″ × 10″   1972

may be said to correspond to the marriage of Heaven and Earth. Without such a marriage there can be no nativity. But just as the imbalance of partners precludes a true marriage, so only a true marriage of intellect and intuition can give birth to the Christ (presupposing the desire for a child in the first place). When this new consciousness is born, however, it transcends the so-called "light of reason," Christ consciousness being a different quality of light altogether. I realize "Christ consciousness" is a loaded expression, but all I mean to imply is the opening of the channel of awareness, and that in itself is entirely a question of degree.

The Christ *is* the channel of awareness, but the channel of awareness to what? Jesus, speaking as the Christ, said, "No man cometh to the Father except by me," so it seems that the channel leads to the Father. The Father, traditionally, is thought of as an old man with a beard who lives in Heaven, but we have been told that the Kingdom of Heaven is within ourselves, so it follows that the Father is within ourselves too.

Now, when I painted those little pictures "by accident," what I did was paint the channel of awareness over and over again; and then, through those channels I found over and over again the image of the bearded old man (45). I realize that the conclusion I have drawn from this sequence of events is subjective in the extreme, but within the context of my own quest I have come to take such clues seriously. In other words, since the channel leads to the Father, I cannot avoid the conclusion that the hermit, or Wise Old Man, *is* the Father; or, if that seems belittling to the Almighty Creator and Sustainer of the Universe, then at least the voice of God in man and woman.

46. HERMIT WITH CAT AND BIRD   40″ × 29″   1972

THE QUEST

I. The Giants II   19″ × 17″   1974

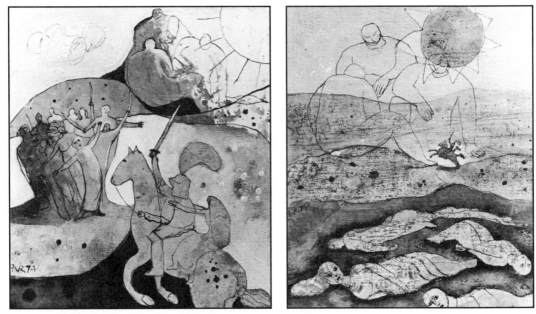

II. THE CRUSADERS III   17″ × 19″   1974

III. THE CRUSADERS IV   15″ × 18″   1974

IV. THE CRUSADERS I   16″ × 11″   1973

V. THE CRUSADERS II   16″ × 18″   1973

VI. FLIGHT   12″ × 10″   1974

VII. THE GIFT I   19″ × 16″   1975

VIII. THE ABYSS   12″ × 16″   1974

IX. THE SECOND MUSE (MEMORY)   83″ × 66″   1972

X. THE DOVE   86″ × 68″   1972

XI. The Channel   67″ × 101″   1972

XII. BYSTANDERS   12″ × 11″   1975

XIII. The Mountaintop 17″ × 19″ 1974

XIV. The Way 18″ × 16″ 1985

XV. THE ENTRANCE TO THE FOREST II   16″ × 12″   1975

XV. The horse symbolizes instinct; the man, intellect; the woman, intuition; the dove, inspiration; the forest, the mind. The man leads the horse and the woman into the forest. This does not bode well, for one cannot hope to discern the truth guided by intellect alone. The dove is soon lost. To enter the forest in such a manner is to court confusion (XVI) and, in all likelihood, a fall (XVII). The fall in question is a fall from grace. The instinct for the Quest is itself a gift of grace, so the horse may be seen to symbolize, not only instinct, but grace too. It is that which carries the man and woman on their journey. They would do well—especially in the early stages—to give the horse its head.

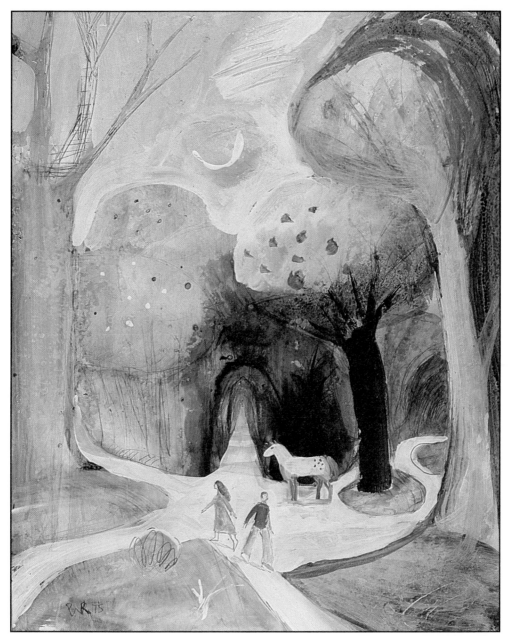

XVI. FOREST PATHS 11″ × 15″ 1975

XVII. Fall   56″ × 80″   1980

XVIII. THE STORM   16″ × 12″   1975

XIX. THE RETURN OF THE DOVE II   17″ × 14″   1975

XX. Gifts   84" × 48"   1985

XX. This picture symbolizes the fulfillment of the promise, "Seek first the kingdom of heaven within, and the rest shall be added unto you." The acceptance of the promise, and the understanding of the principle behind it (best summed up in John XV: 1-8) would go a long way towards abolishing poverty and starvation from the face of the Earth. As it is, most of us believe that we are subject to the whims of the economy. Fearing what it may or may not do to us, we treat the economy as though it were a god. There is nothing new in this. It is simply a new form of idolatry, for the economy is the modern equivalent of a golden calf, its adherents idolators whether they like it or not.

Material lack may have sparked my own quest, but the fact remains that little or no progress can be made if one's goal is merely to achieve material well-being; the kingdom must be sought for its own sake—"the rest" follows. Or does it? Can the promise really be taken literally? Considering the totally haphazard nature of an artist's income, I have been in a good position to prove—at least to my own satisfaction—that "the rest" is indeed "added." This being so, I would suggest that the Quest presents a practical solution—perhaps the only practical solution—to the problems of poverty and starvation generally. So, bearing in mind that the Quest is a journey that can only be taken by individuals, what hope is there of solving those problems universally?

Many people feel that, as a race, we have reached an impasse, a cul-de-sac, which means that the way is blocked and there appears to be no way out—in other words, they feel road-

less—and I have no doubt that the Gnostics were right when they suggested that this feeling of roadlessness indicates a person's readiness for the Quest. Since more people than ever before are suffering from this feeling, it follows that more people than ever before are ready for the Quest. Many have already begun. Indeed there is hope.

XXI. THE COMET II   10″ × 10″   1978

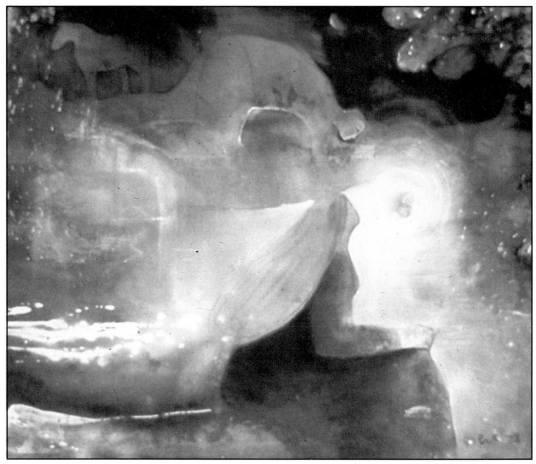

XXII. THE POOL II   50″ × 43″   1978

XXII. *The pool symbolizes the unconscious. They look in the pool and see the Light. It is their own reflection. They* are *the Light. When the Light is found within, it manifests without (XXIII).*

XXIII. SUNRISE III   66″ × 70″   1980

XXIV. METAMORPHOSIS   82″ × 66″   1980

XXV. The Second Baptism II   60″ × 78″   1982

XXV. *The Spirit of Truth alights on the man. The woman holds the fruit of the Tree of Life. Heaven is now their Reality, for consciousness has become a channel for the Light of God to shine on Earth.*

XXVI. ASCENSION   12″ × 14″   1975

FIVE
THE CHANNEL

For reasons that will become apparent in a moment, I want to return briefly to Mojacar.

When I first arrived in Mojacar there was not a single restaurant in town, let alone a hotel, and since the mayor of Mojacar hoped to develop the area as a tourist resort, during the time I was there much building went on. The mayor's plan stood scant chance of success, however, and for one good reason —there was not enough water. Several wells were dug, but, being near the sea, the water was brackish. Though the obvious source of good water was in the mountains behind Mojacar, it was not the Mojaceros who finally realized this, but the mayor of Garucha—Garucha being the local fishing port six kilometers up the coast. There was no love lost between the mountainfolk of Mojacar and the fisherfolk of Garucha, and it was in secrecy that the Garucheros began mining into the mountain behind Mojacar in quest of water.

Now, when I say that there was not enough water, what I really mean is that the people no longer knew how to harness water. In the old days there had been a highly sophisticated irrigation system, and the evidence for it confronted the townsfolk every day. Between the mountains and the sea, and not far from the base of the mountain crowned by the jumble of white cubes that was the town, stood a symmetrical pyramid with a flat top, roughly one hundred feet tall. I presumed it to be an odd natural formation, and no one gave me reason to believe otherwise, until one day I climbed it. At the top I found an oblong hole and, peering in, discovered the whole top of the pyramid to be a huge barrel-shaped cistern. The Arabs must have built it, or perhaps the Romans before them.. At any rate, it was an impressive monument to past intelligence which, by comparison, made what now transpired the more pathetic.

The people of Garucha mined a long way into the mountain before they found water, and when they did they were ecstatic. They let off fireworks to celebrate, and people came from far and wide to stare at the little stream issuing from the tunnel. Every day the volume of water was measured, every day it got bigger, and the crowds that came to stare got bigger, until the tunnel in the mountain gushed like a huge fire hose and the water crashed down the mountainside, sweeping away bushes and topsoil and running, eventually, straight out to sea. And this went on for days, and whether anyone thought about what to do with all the water I do not know. But then some of the small springs that had watered the orange groves for centuries dried up, and it was noticed that the great spring at the foot of the mountain was running less strongly than usual. Eventually there was an outcry against the people of Garucha, and in the end the tunnel had to be blown up.

Southeastern New Mexico is, for the most part, as arid as the province of Almeria. The valley in which we live is an exception, however. Seen from the air, it is a narrow ribbon of green, twisting its way between endless, rolling, sun-baked hills; but as we live in the valley, it is our world. The life of the valley is entirely dependent on a small river, one of the few in New Mexico that flows throughout the year. A complex system of irrigation channels, leading from the river, brings water to the pastures and apple orchards. The valley is a lush oasis and, together with the conscientious farmers who tend it, symbolizes something very different from the fable of human folly I witnessed in Mojacar.*

In 1974 I was commissioned to paint a mural for the Museum of Texas Tech University in Lubbock, which is a center for the study of arid and semi-arid land and water problems generally. The president of the university told me that if he were to sum up the subject of the mural he wanted in one word, it would be "Water." He then drew up a list of places for me to go to in search of data: Sand Dunes National Park in southern Colorado; Monument Valley

---

It would be unfair not to mention the fact that, since writing the above, I have learned that the Mojaceros have solved their water problem. They pipe it many miles from a neighboring mountain range, and Mojacar has become a flourishing tourist resort after all.

47. HEADGATE, detail of mural   16′ × 10′ (40′ × 17′)   1974

and Zion National Park in Utah; the Mojave desert in California; and the Chihuahuan desert in Mexico. I dutifully set out and got as far as Colorado. During the night, which I spent in my car, it occurred to me that the whole trip was crazy. Why, if the mural was to be about water, had I been sent to the only places in North America where one was almost guaranteed not to find any? The next day I went home, and the following day decided to make the subject of the mural a small crib dam that had been built across the creek less than a mile down the valley from where we lived.

Now, just above the dam was a headgate controlling the flow of water to some land belonging to a good friend of mine and, since I wanted a figure in the composition somewhere, I asked my friend to pose for me in the act of clearing debris from the grill of the headgate with a hoe, which he did (47). It was this incident that gave me the idea for a series of paintings I called *The Hermit and the Headgate*. The more I thought about it, the more the symbolism of river, headgate, ditches, pastures, etc., intrigued me. All the pictures in the eventual series derived (in a loose sense, because I painted them all from memory) from different places in the valley, but they were given continuity as a series by virtue of the fact that either the hermit or headgate, or both, were included in all of them (48 and 49).

What can be deduced from all this? First, that the ways of the farmers in the valley present an interesting contrast to the ways of the people of Mojacar. The Mojaceros needed water, but although there was plenty of it, they did not know how to channel it. On the other hand the methods of the farmers in the valley symbolize the way things ought to, and can, work.

Second, we do not go to deserts to find water, even if university presidents tell us to; the water we need is close at hand all the time.

Third, the word "headgate" is suggestive. By means of the headgate we draw water from the river so that our pastures may be lush and our orchards fruitful. The hermit regulates the flow, but only through our own channels can He do what has to be done.

48. Hermit and Headgate   17″ × 14″   1975

49. THE RIVER   86″ × 48″   1975

50. THE FLIGHT INTO EGYPT   9″ × 9″   1972

SIX

FIRE AND WATER

Shortly after the Nativity, Mary and Joseph, to escape the wrath of Herod, fled with the infant Christ to Egypt (50). This was no historical accident; it was a necessary part of the myth. When the Christ is newborn in consciousness it is vulnerable, and the world, or material consciousness, like Herod, will do its best to destroy it. If it is to have a chance to grow, reticence is essential. In other words, when you plant a seed in the ground you do not dig it up to see how it is growing because, if you do, it will die. The newborn Christ is like a seed planted in the ground of human consciousness. Provided it is not exposed to the world too soon, it will grow in strength, manifesting to an ever increasing extent "the will of my Father."

At least that is the aim, but even Jesus was tempted. The devil may have addressed him deferentially as "Son of God," but it is an interesting fact that every temptation was one calculated to appeal to Jesus as ego as opposed to Jesus as the Christ. As the Christ incarnate, Jesus was by that time invulnerable, but we can hardly lay claim to any such invulnerability ourselves. The ego is full of tricks and dies hard. It is the one thing that can prevent the growth of Christ consciousness, and it is no doubt for this reason that the problem of ego has spawned more myths and legends than any other aspect of the Quest. Common to most of these myths are the elements, fire and water.

So far I have mentioned the symbol of water only in its life-sustaining aspect—as the water of life, or inspiration of the Spirit—but water can be destructive, too. Fire, of course, shares the same two properties. Volumes could be written on the symbolism of these two mutually antagonistic elements, but I shall confine what I have to say to those aspects that are reflected in *The Quest*.

105

These are the trials by water and fire and the baptisms with water and fire. The trials correspond to the destructive properties of water and fire, the baptisms to the life-sustaining.

When one speaks of trials by water and fire, certain cruel legal practices of the Middle Ages and the dunking of witches come to mind, but such things are, thank God, things of the past. Perhaps these practices were dim echoes of ancient myths such as the pre-Christian Irish myth of Conn-eda,* which dates from an age when trials by fire and water were properly understood; but of one thing we may be certain—such trials were never meant to be taken literally. As for baptism, literal baptism with—or in—water continues, and most Christians are aware that John the Baptist spoke of a second baptism: "I indeed baptize you with water unto repentence: but he that cometh. . .shall baptize you with the Holy Ghost, and with fire." No one supposes that he meant fire literally any more than anyone believes that the sign of the cross made on the baby's forehead with a finger dipped in water actually does anything to the baby. Such words, such actions, are of course symbolic—but symbolic of what?.

Baptism, whether with water or with fire, is meaningful only within the context of the Quest and, as with anything concerning the Quest, both sorts

---

*I mention the story of Conn-eda because the imagery of that myth and the imagery of The Quest have much in common. In fact my discovery of the Conn-eda myth removed any lingering doubts I may have had concerning the existence of a collective unconscious.

First, Conn-eda was named after his father, King Conn of Ireland, and his mother, Queen Eda of Brittany. Therefore, like the man and woman of The Quest, the name Conn-eda symbolizes both the male and female aspects of one psyche.

Second, Conn-eda rides a magic horse. Initially he lets the horse take him wherever it wants to go.

Third, Conn-eda and the horse descend into the waters of a lake that turn to mist as they enter them. There they encounter three serpents that have to be propitiated. The serpents symbolize the supposedly deadly power of the water. The three giants of The Quest theme symbolize the seemingly deadly power of evil, but just as the waters turn to mist when Conn-eda enters them, so the giants prove to be a mirage.

Finally, Conn-eda and the horse have to cross a burning mountain. In The Quest the man and woman run a gauntlet of volcanoes. For an account of the Conn-eda myth, see Heinrich Zimmer, The King and the Corpse (Bollingen Series XI, Princeton: 1948).

51. THE SECOND BAPTISM I   66″ × 80″   1982

52. Cataclysm I   11" × 15"   1975

of baptism have to do with evolving consciousness. The basic idea behind the symbolism is extremely simple: we have to shake off old beliefs before we can accept new ones. Ego, or material, consciousness has to be left behind before we can enter the Kingdom, and the Kingdom implies a new state of conscious-ness—Christ consciousness. So it is a question of the rejection of something in the first place and the affirmation of something else in the second. The rejec-tion, the denial or washing away of ego consciousness, is the water baptism, whereas the affirmation of our real relationship to God, the acceptance of our true identity as a child of God, is the fire baptism (51). There has to be a letting-go before there can be a taking-hold.

But before there can be a letting-go, it has to be brought home to one pre-cisely what one is letting go of; otherwise, the act is meaningless. Hence the necessity of trials and, inevitably, tribulations—for the two go hand in hand. Likewise, even after the rejection of material values the affirmation of one's true relationship to God will also be meaningless, and possibly even dangerous, unless one is first purged of ego. So after the material cleansing there has to be a spiritual cleansing, and this is what is known as the trial by fire. Trials and baptisms seem to go in cycles, and I suspect they continue as long as the Quest itself.

I included fire and water symbolism in my paintings long before I under-stood what it really meant. In 1971 I came close to the mark, however. Search-ing for an image to symbolize the destruction of ego consciousness prior to the attainment of oneness, I borrowed Velikovsky's scenario: as the comet approaches Earth, the seas stand on end and volcanoes erupt, which was my way of saying that as God becomes more of a reality in one's inner life, upheavals should be expected in one's outer life (52, 53, 54). Such trials are part of the tempering process that has to take place in order for consciousness to expand safely. The cataclysm paintings symbolize this tempering process, but long before I painted the first tidal waves and volcanoes I had already unwit-tingly used the symbols of water and fire in my painting. In the two cases I have in mind, both pictures symbolized the purging of ego: a rejection of a limited and finite sense of self in the first case (a water picture) and the affirmation, albeit ironical, of one's true identity in the second (a fire picture).

It was certainly no accident that the first painting of the *Life of Christ* series depicted the panic-stricken apostles adrift in a boat on the stormy sea (22). When I began that painting back in 1960 I had been identifying strongly with ego and had suffered the consequences. I had fallen into the first ego trap: the victim trap. I had only been rescued from that victim condition by making a conscious effort to know the truth—in other words, by trying to concentrate on the Christ as the true nature of my being—and this recognition had opened the channel of awareness. As a result, I had again heard some words spoken that in one sentence gave me the solution to the whole problem I was confronting. What I had to do was easy after that, but what I did was something that would normally be judged good. What actually happened was due to the activity of the Christ, but under such circumstances it is easy to fail to give credit where it is due and even easier to take it for oneself. Before one knows what is happening, one is thinking, "*I* am good," and there one is, caught in the second trap—what I call the "saint trap." This second ego trap, because it is more insidious, is more deadly than the first.

The process of extricating myself from this trap, and the symbolic cleansing by fire that that process entailed, was reflected in a picture I painted the following year in Mojacar. The idea for the painting came from the image of a local deity called Indalo, whom the Mojaceros sometimes painted on the outside of their houses. He was a little man standing with his legs astride and his arms outstretched, with what I was told was a rainbow described over his head, joining hand to hand. The image resembled a mushroom, and it was this thought that led to my thinking in terms of mushroom clouds and their sinister implications. It was the time of the Cuban missile crisis and, although I felt far removed from the problems of the world, I was well aware of what was going on. Feeling compelled to make some statement about it, I realized that Indalo presented me with a ready-made image.

So I painted this picture of Man incinerating himself and called it *Bomb Image*. Merely to fill a space, I gave the man a fiery aura, and then some impulse made me write on the painting in crude lettering, "Oh, Mummy, I've got a halo." I was, of course, aware at the time that my reason for writing those silly words had nothing to do with the impulse that had led me to paint the picture

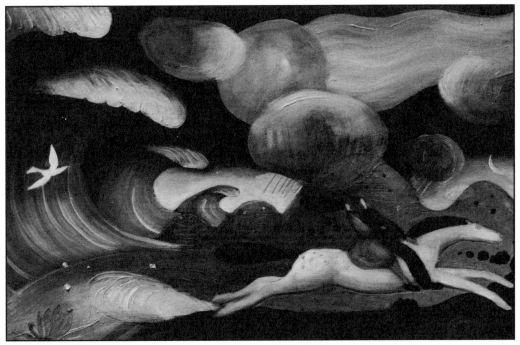

53. TRIAL BY WATER   25″ × 16″   1985

54. TRIAL BY FIRE   25″ × 16″   1985

in the first place—the reason was entirely personal. I was suffering from what in Jungian terms would be called ego inflation. The ego was claiming for itself the attributes of the Self, but at least I realized this in a dim way and liked no part of it—which is why, in self-contempt, I painted those words on that picture. Until I could rid myself of the notion that I was good, like the man in my paintings, I would continue to burn in fire.

Since those days I have long since given up the idea that I am good—I have done things that have given me plenty of reason to believe otherwise—so this ego trap no longer poses a threat. But by this I do not mean to imply that I now believe myself to be bad. I think of myself as neither good nor bad, but, like everyone else in this world, a mixture of the two. Such a realization is an important step, because without it the light and dark in human nature can never be integrated. Unless the light and dark are integrated, oneness remains a pipe dream.

But *how* are the opposites integrated? Perhaps art can provide a clue. The integration of opposites is, after all, the daily concern of artists, unity being the primary goal of the creative process.

55. THE FOOL   19″ × 16″   1971

112

PART TWO

The Real World consists in a balanced adjustment of opposing tendencies. Behind the strife between opposites there lies a hidden harmony or attunement which is the world.

Heraclitus

56. SUNRISE I   13″ × 10″   1974

SEVEN
THE CREATIVE PROCESS

A wise man once said that, "Harmony is essentially a resolution of irreducible tensions."[10] This might come as a surprise to some people, but it would be no surprise to the artist. Harmony implies unity and unity is a prerequisite of any work of art. In order to achieve unity the artist, whether painter, poet, or composer, follows a fine line between pairs of conflicting opposites.

The precise nature of these pairs of opposites differs from artist to artist, but speaking for myself, and as a painter, I find I am constantly torn between classicism and romanticism, deliberation and spontaneity, care and carelessness, reason and intuition, boldness and tentativeness. If I go too far in any one direction something is usually lost: too classical, too cerebral, and my painting becomes sterile; too romantic, and it tends towards sentimentality or—worse—whimsy; too careful, and I lose vitality; too careless, and I court chaos, and so on.

Painting is a process of continual decision making. Sometimes the decisions are conscious and sometimes they are unconscious, but every time a painter puts brush to canvas a choice must be made between opposite possibilities: paint can be light or dark, warm or cool, thick or thin, rough or smooth—the list can be extended almost ad infinitum. The power of the painting depends on how the artist handles the tensions inherent in these pairs of opposites.

Whether simple or complex, bold or subtle, a painting is fundamentally a pattern of relationships. A work is completed only when every mark is related to every other mark, whether or not it is unified being the principle yardstick

115

of success or failure. It is a difficult process. Torn as one is between all manner of opposing tensions, it is often a painful process too. Furthermore, the Muse is fickle, excellence elusive, the rewards uncertain. And yet there will always be artists. All things considered, one might well wonder why.

Art school taught me a lot about the "hows" of art, but nothing about the "whys." If the teachers knew why people bothered to paint pictures they were not telling the students, and it never occurred to any of us to ask. Art was sold in galleries like expensive furniture and if, as was obvious, there was more to it than that, I would nevertheless have found it difficult to say precisely why. It was only after I left art school that the question began to nag at me: "What is art really *for?*"

57. Cardplayers   40″ × 30″   1956

In 1956, the year that I left art school, I read Roger Fry's *Vision and Design* and came on these words in an essay on William Blake:

> The essential power of pictorial as of all other arts lies in its use of a fundamental and universal symbolism, and whoever has the instinct for this can convey his ideas, though possessed of only the most rudimentary knowledge of the actual forms of nature; while he who has it not can by no accumulation of observed facts add anything to the spiritual treasure of mankind.[11]

Those words were both an exhortation and a warning to me, and gave me my first clue to the purpose and function of art. To add to "the spiritual treasure of mankind" seemed a worthy, if presumptuous, ambition, but in 1956 I had no idea what the creation of "fundamental and universal symbolism" entailed. I had vague notions of lying on my back in a meadow, dreaming up imagery as I watched the clouds go by—which perhaps was just as well, because, had I been blessed with foresight, I might have backed away. As it was, I naively set my sights and in due course, in the purposeful, though invariably surprising, ways that I have described, my imagery began to evolve.

Incidentally, that same book had ended with these words:

> As to the value of the aesthetic emotion . . . it seems to be as remote from actual life and its practical utilities as the most useless mathematical theory. One can only say that those who experience it feel it to have a peculiar quality of "reality" which makes it a matter of infinite importance in their lives. Any attempt I might make to explain this would probably land me in the depths of mysticism. On the edge of that gulf I stop.[12]

Fry was one of the chief advocates of modern art in England before and immediately after the First World War. He must have known his cause would not be helped were he to be branded a mystic, so he can hardly be blamed for stopping on the edge of that gulf. However, his words betrayed the fact that he did know what art was for, even if he had decided not to tell his readers.

A year or two later I discovered the writings of Ouspensky. He had some cogent things to say about art; in the space of a few sentences he summed up not only what art ought to be, but what it ought not to be. He began:

If we try to define the significance of the four ways of the spiritual life of humanity, we see, first of all, that they fall into two categories. Philosophy and science are intellectual ways; religion and art, emotional ways.[13]

So it seemed that as one of the four ways of "the spiritual life of humanity," art was an approach to Reality—but how and why? Having summarized the purpose and function of philosophy, science, and religion, Ouspensky went on:

Art is based on emotional understanding, on the feeling of the Unknown which lies behind the visible and the tangible, and on creative power, the power, that is, to reconstruct in visible or audible forms the artist's sensations, feelings, visions and moods, and especially a certain fugitive sensation, which is in fact the feeling of the harmonious interconnection and oneness of *everything* and the feeling of the "soul" of things and phenomena. Like science and philosophy, art is a definite *way of knowledge*. The artist, in creating, learns much that he did not know before. But an art which does not reveal mysteries, which does not lead to the sphere of the Unknown, does not yield new knowledge, is a parody of art, and still more often it is not even a parody, but simply a commerce or an industry.[14]

By the time I read those words I had already discovered the key images of oneness and separateness and thought I knew what Ouspensky was talking about. My painting was indeed a "way of knowledge," but in so far as I thought that my quest for imagery was itself the "way of knowledge" Ouspensky was talking about, I was missing half the point. Ouspensky was talking not only about *what* one paints, but *how* one paints; not only about content, but about process too.

This fact was eventually brought home to me in 1969. I had been asked to give a lecture on art in our local town and thought I would try to answer the question, "What is art for?," but in my attempt to get my thoughts in order, I soon ran into problems. By now I knew from experience that in order to make a painting work, content had to take second place. In fact whenever I had what I thought was a good idea for a picture that was other than a good idea about *painting*, the picture was almost certainly doomed to failure; but as yet I was blind to the conclusions I should have been able to draw from this. That art was a "way of knowledge" I had no doubt; that there was more to it than a quest

58. PORTRAIT OF JENNY   19″ × 24″   1958

59. SELF-PORTRAIT   12″ × 14″   1959

for "fundamental and universal symbolism" I was certain; but what exactly was this other factor?

I had recently been given a copy of Bertrand Russell's *Wisdom of the West*, but since I find most philosophy heavy going and generally unrewarding, I was in no hurry to read it. It was beautifully illustrated, however, and one day I was glancing through it when these words by Heraclitus caught my eye:

> The Real World consists in a balanced adjustment of opposing tendencies. Behind the strife between opposites there lies a hidden harmony or attune-ment which is the world.[15]

It appeared that the Real World to Heraclitus was what the Kingdom of Heaven is to the Christian mystic, or what Nirvana is to the Buddhist.

I was well aware that Heraclitus was not talking about art, and yet in those two brief sentences I found the answer I was looking for; because what is a work of art, whether a painting, poem, piece of sculpture, symphony, or building, other than a "balanced adjustment of opposing tendencies"? Painters, for instance, whether they know it or not, in their attempt to balance the lights and darks, the hot colors and cool colors, as they try to relate all the parts of the painting to the whole, are—if successful—painting their own version, or vision, of the world of "harmony or attunement;" in other words, they are

60. PORTRAIT OF DEBORAH   8″ × 12″   1963

painting the Real World that Heraclitus said lies behind our self-created world of "strife between opposites." This being so, I realized that it is the creative process itself, more than anything else, that justifies art as a way of knowledge, whereas the finished work of art is tangible evidence that the mystics are right —that oneness is indeed attainable via the dualities inherent in human experience.

No wonder, therefore, that those who experience the aesthetic emotion "feel it to have a peculiar quality of 'reality' which makes it a matter of infinite importance in their lives"; no wonder that this emotion seems "remote from actual life and its practical utilities," because the concern of art has nothing to do with this—the concern of art is with the Real World. The painter paints Reality.

∽

When I entered art school I thought that I knew how to draw, but the first thing I learned was that not only did I not know how to draw—I did not know how to *see*. In our life-drawing classes we were taught to see the human figure as a whole, and by so doing to relate the various parts of the body to one another truthfully on the paper so that the whole body had convincing form, rhythm, and direction in space. If one was unable to see in this way, one was simply unable to draw.

In drawing the human figure we were relating the parts of the figure to itself, the space around the figure being largely ignored, but in painting a picture our problems expanded to the four edges of the canvas. Only in our second year were we allowed to paint. We then had not only to contend with the problems of drawing, but also with those of composition and color. Nevertheless, the basic problem remained the same; it was still a question of relationships, the only difference being that there were now more of them to consider. Every line, form, and area of color had to be related to every other line, form, and color in order to arrive at a completed whole that had unity. Unity was the goal, but this was impossible to achieve unless one kept an eye on the entire composition all the time.

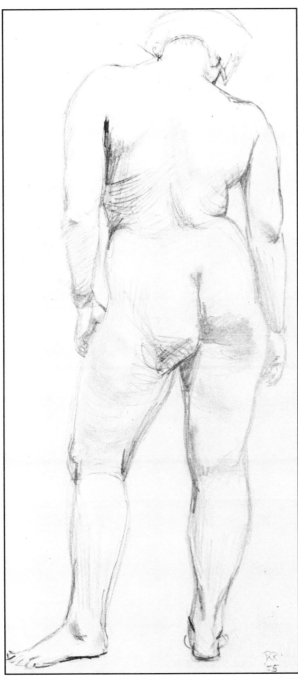

62. MALE NUDE I   1955

61. FEMALE NUDE   1955

63. MALE NUDE II   1955

64. PORTRAIT OF GILLIAN   20″ × 25″   1979

65. RIO HONDO   18″ × 24″   1964

66. ARROYO   24″ × 18″   1964

67. RANCH ROAD   30″ × 21″   1964

68. PORTRAIT OF JAMES   30″ × 48″   1956

69. DRILLING RIG, PRUDHOE BAY   30″ × 22″   1969

70. DRAWWORKS AND SWIVEL   30″ × 22″   1969

71. "Christmas Tree"   22" × 30"   1969

Unfortunately, as most art students soon learn, it is all too easy to get stuck on a problem involving one small part of a painting and, with a sort of tunnel vision, to worry at it continually, becoming blind to the rest of the picture in the process. The consequences of this are predictable enough, but the trap is easy to fall into and remains something that artists have to beware of all their working lives. Often I have worked all day on a certain part of a painting, and gone to bed confident that that particular part was just right, only to get up in the morning and see with a fresh eye that that part, perfect in itself, destroyed the unity of the whole. It is a question of focus, and focus on any one part of a painting at the expense of the rest leads to much waste of time, energy, and paint. Unless one's focus is on the whole painting all the time, one cannot expect it to work.

These facts are basic to the creative process and of course apply equally to all art forms. They are the fundamentals of what one learns at art school, and I am certain that it never occurred to any of us that there was anything spiritual about it. If one wanted to paint well, this is what one had to do. It was purely pragmatic.

Now, whereas at art school we were told what to do and what not to do if we wanted to paint a good picture, religion tells us what to do and what not to do if we want to live a good life. As I shall attempt to demonstrate in a moment, the two sets of instructions are remarkably similar, and this led me to the conclusion that the same laws that apply to art apply to the creative process we call life. The only difference is that at art school we attached no ethical connotations to what we were told to do; it was simply a question of what worked and what did not. Certainly, there were good ways and bad ways of trying to solve a problem, but we only considered them good or bad according to whether or not they solved it. People have been trying to solve their problems for thousands of years, but no sooner is one solved than a worse one seems to come along. Painters are familiar with this pattern. You change one part of the picture and seem to get it right, but in the process you make another part wrong and then you have to change that too, and so on, round and round. When that happens there can only be one reason: you have fallen into the trap; you have lost sight of the composition as a whole.

72. HERMIT PAINTING A BIRD   19″ × 16″   1975

All great religious teachers have done their best to correct our failure to see. Now, at first sight there may seem to be little or no connection between the words I am about to quote and the process I have just been talking about, but I ask you to bear with me. Christ gave the world two commandments to supersede the Ten Commandments of the Old Testament; they were as follows:

> The first of all the commandments is, Hear, O Israel; The Lord our God is one Lord: And thou shalt love the Lord thy God with all thy heart, and with all thy soul, and with all thy mind, and with all thy strength...And the second is like, namely this, Thou shalt love thy neighbour as thyself. There are none other commandments greater than these.

131

73. HERMIT AT SUNRISE   8″ × 7″   1972

I am aware that these commandments are so loaded with inherited connotations that it is difficult not to think, on the one hand, of a bad-tempered old man somewhere up there in the sky whom we have never met but whom we are unreasonably supposed to love and, on the other, of taking a nice hot meal round to poor Mrs. Jones next door because she is laid up with the flu. This is because most of us fail to question what Jesus meant by God and one's neighbor. In fact he taught, as Native Americans believe, that God is everywhere and in everything. In St. Thomas' gospel, speaking as the Christ, he is quoted as saying, "Split the stick, you will find me there. Lift the stone and there I am"; but this teaching was lost to Christianity until the Thomas gospel was discovered in 1945. So God, far from being an old man in the sky, is the Whole, whereas one's neighbor, far from being merely the person who lives next door, is everyone and everything that exists, together with oneself, within the context of that Whole. We are all part of God.

There is a parable in the twenty-fifth chapter of Matthew which ends like this: "Verily I say unto you, in as much as ye have done it unto one of the least of these thy brethren, ye have done it unto me." In the parable it is the king speaking and the king is God. So whatever is done to one's neighbor—the part—is also done to God—the Whole. Nevertheless, even though the parable implies that, in a sense, God and one's neighbor are one and the same, all the emphasis was put on the *first* commandment. One might say that ethically this seems reasonable enough, but the real reason for this emphasis only became apparent to me in the light of my experience as a painter.

Each part of a painting, each line of a poem, each bar of a symphony is important not only because the complete work of art cannot exist without it but because what you—as painter, poet, or composer—do to each part, line, or bar is what you are doing to the whole painting, poem, or symphony. However, it would be absurd to suppose that any artist is going to consider one part of a composition more important than the whole composition. Likewise, one does not really think that one's neighbor, the part, is more important than God, the Whole. But whereas the artist soon learns the *necessity* of keeping his focus on the work of art as a whole all the time, in everyday human experience our focus tends to be exclusively on the parts. We continue to struggle with the problems inherent in those parts, not realizing that by so doing we can never hope to achieve harmony and attunement. The first commandment was first for a good reason.

To put it another way: It is true of art, as of life, that we can never hope to solve our problems by participating in the strife between opposites. The artist knows this only too well. He also knows that, provided he concentrates on the painting as a whole, the warring elements in the design are soon resolved. Likewise in life, by focusing on the Whole and loving the Whole with all our heart, soul, mind, and strength, the warring elements in human reality are sooner or later resolved too. It is all a question of focus and of love.

∽

That love is essential to the creative process is something all artists know, but rarely talk about. There are three forms of love—physical, mental, and spiritual—and all three are essential to artists.

I remember the Polish artist, Joseph Herman, coming to St. Martin's one day and speaking to us in the student commonroom. He urged us to love our paint. We should love our paint so much that we should feel like rubbing our fingers in it first thing every morning; almost, he said, we should feel like eating it. Herman was advocating sensuality rather than spirituality, Eros rather than Agape, and such love is of course physical in nature. Whether applied to the canvas with passion or with delicate sensitivity, artists must always handle their paint with love. Unless the paint is loved, the paint, and hence the painting, will lack quality.

Whatever artists paint, or poets write, is necessarily born in the mind or, in the case of painters, in the mind's eye. Whatever artists see in the mind's eye is called their "vision." It is the Muse that gives birth to this vision in the conscious mind of artists, the Muse being the personification of their unconscious mind, their source of inspiration. Artists may find this source of inspiration in the physical world in, for instance, the way the light strikes a grove of trees or in a certain relationship between objects—there is no knowing where or when

74. SUNRISE II   15″ × 16″   1975

the Muse will show herself—or in the mind, in an abstract idea or even a vision; but unless there is something to excite their passionate interest, artists will have nothing worth saying. This passionate interest is mental love. Mental love is essential to the creative process, because without it there is no vision, and without vision there are no artists.

When looking at paintings, one can tell at a glance whether or not the artists in question love their subject matter (*what* they paint) and their medium (what they paint *with*), but to love the subject matter and to love the medium is not enough. One can also tell at a glance whether or not the composition is resolved—whether or not it works—and in order for a painting to work artists have to love the creative process itself (*how* they paint). This implies that artists must love not only each and every part of the composition but, more importantly, the composition as a whole. This love for the composition as a whole is comparable to spiritual love, for spiritual love implies a love for God, and a love for God *is* a love for the Whole. But the analogy can be taken further.

In relationships between men and women, whereas physical and mental love, if spurned, often turn into their opposite, hatred, this is not true of spiritual love. From my own experience I can vouch for the fact that when two people share a love of truth or a spiritual love, which is the same as a love of God, it creates a bond that is indissoluble. It makes no difference what fate may have in store for that relationship—the love for the other person remains unchanged. This is because the love in question is unconditional. Unconditional love, which is true spiritual love, knows no opposite because it is love without judgment. In other words, unconditional love transcends duality. It is, of course, the artist's goal to transcend duality, but if unconditional love is love without judgment, at first glance it is here that the analogy may seem to break down.

One might well wonder what an artist is doing when painting a picture other than making continual judgments—this color is wrong, this form too big, that tone too dark, etc.—but the problem is more semantic than real, because what the artist is really saying is, "This color is wrong, I'll use that one instead,"

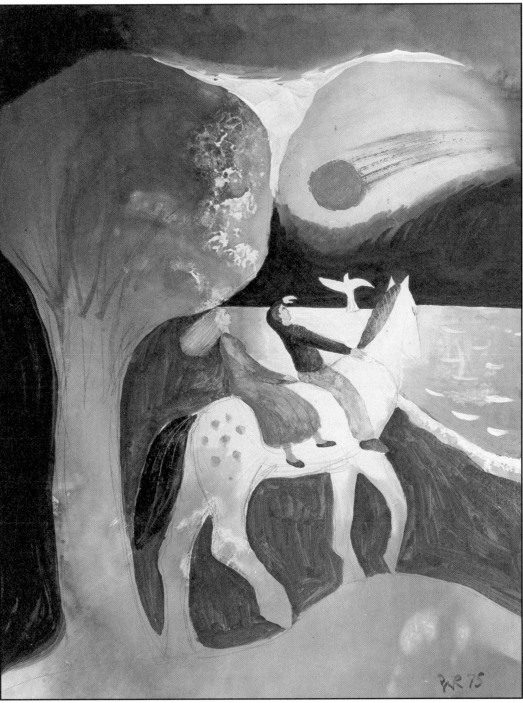

75. THE COMET I   12″ × 15″   1975

and this is not so much a question of judgment as of choice. There is a big difference between choice and judgment. Whereas we tend to think of judgment in terms of moral judgment, choice suggests no such thing. As I said earlier, "At art school we attached no ethical connotations to what we were told to do; it was simply a question of what worked and what did not." To make a painting work the artist makes choices all the time, and a bad choice is merely something to be avoided. So, insofar as an artist makes choices and not judgments, the love for the work is truly unconditional and the analogy holds good to the end.

To sum up: An artist transcending duality on canvas is testifying to spiritual reality, and that is the function of an artist. It is, of course, far easier to transcend duality on canvas than it is to transcend duality in life; far easier to make a painting work than it is to make a life work; far easier to love paint than to love people. I am not suggesting that the problem is the same, but that it follows the same pattern, for the basic problem of painting (and of all the arts) reflects the basic problem of life, which is how to attain oneness. But art does more than mimic life; art enhances the *quality* of life, and it does so partly by revealing the nature of the Real World, and partly by showing us how we may become part of that Real World. How does it do this? It shows us by analogy. The nature of the Real World is oneness, and oneness is the hallmark of all successful works of art. There can be no oneness in a work of art, however, unless the opposites are integrated, and there can be no integration of opposites unless artists are prepared to focus their attention in the particular manner already described. As I have tried to show, this focused attention is necessarily a *loving* focus, the love in question being unconditional. As in art, so in life. If we would transcend "the strife between opposites," if we would unlock the door to the Real World, unconditional love is the key. Properly understood as a question of focus, unconditional love *is* the creative process.

76. THE POOL I   50″ × 46″   1973

77. RIVER CROSSING II   102″ × 120″   1983

EIGHT

A PAINTER'S PERSPECTIVE

I hope it is clear by now why, and in what sense, art is "a definite way of knowledge." Artists, in creating, do indeed learn much they did not know before—but once acquired, what do they *do* with this knowledge. Do they just file it away? To do so would make nonsense of the very purpose and function of art, which is to enhance the quality of life. The sensible thing, surely, would be to apply that knowledge to the problems of life because, if we are to solve those problems before it is too late, worldly knowledge, or so-called "common sense," is no longer enough. What the world desperately needs is spiritual knowledge, or vision. Since it is spiritual knowledge that artists acquire in the practice of the creative process, perhaps it is time for them to share that knowledge. Perhaps, from their own perspective, they can provide some badly needed vision.

All artists have a unique vision of their own to offer, without which they would not be artists. They express this vision in their work, and hence share it with all who see it. It is their own special way of seeing, their own personal vision of the Real World. But there is another facet of an artist's vision—one that is usually taken for granted—that all artists share. This second facet implies a more literal, less personal interpretation of the word "vision" than that usually intended when one speaks of "an artist's vision," but nevertheless it still implies a special way of seeing and, for the artist, this special way of seeing is the prerequisite of success. I am referring to the basic requirement of the creative process: the artist's ability to keep the whole composition constantly in mind while working on the parts, the whole composition being the artist's overriding concern. I have already pointed out the similarity between this dual focus and that advocated by Christ in the two commandments. In fact the two equate precisely, for the two commandments are the *rules* of the creative process. Whether in art or life, the same rules apply, for the simple reason that life *is* art, or should be. The trouble is that, whereas artists soon learn that they have to abide by the rules or fail, in life few seem to have learned that lesson.

Instead, to quote Robert Graves, "Though the West is nominally Christian, we have come to be governed, in practice, by the unholy triumdivate of Pluto, god of wealth, Apollo, god of science, and Mercury, god of thieves. To make matters worse, dissension and jealousy rage openly between these three, with Mercury and Pluto blackguarding each other, while Apollo wields the atomic bomb as if it were a thunderbolt."[16] Pluto, Apollo, and Mercury are the masks currently worn by the Three Lords, who, in their present state of evolution, are the Three Lords of *Materialism*. And so the parts of the Whole compete amongst themselves for dominance and, in the midst of "the strife between opposites," the Whole is forgotten. This, of course, is contrary to the

78. THE THREE LORDS OF MATERIALISM II   62″ × 46″   1978

rules of the creative process. In fact, so persistently have we broken those rules that our materialism is now like a disease in its final stages, for it threatens the very survival of the race.

Our materialism is most evident in the fact that we rely solely on material power for our safety and security. Lacking faith in God, we have put our faith in the Bomb. Not that this is anything new; human beings have always put their faith in material power, the Bomb being merely the modern equivalent of the caveman's club. What *is* new is that we now have the power to annihilate not only the human race, but most of the other life-forms on this planet as well. In view of this fact, it is surely time to question the wisdom of putting our faith in such power. Yet faith in material power remains the prevailing wisdom. We continue to sink the resources of the nation into more and more weapons, ever increasing our capability for mass murder—and all for what? For freedom?

Freedom is an inner condition, and when it is found within, it manifests itself without. In this country we all think of ourselves as free, but our freedom is skin deep. We are not really free at all and it is partly because of this fact—the world being one body—that the canker of tyranny has spread as far as it has. If we would have freedom in the world, we must free ourselves. I am reminded of Michelangelo's slaves emerging half-finished from the stone, struggling to be free, not only of their chains, but—or so it would appear—from the stone itself. The stone is our own self-made "reality," the chains human consciousness, and we are the slaves, slaves to our own beliefs and fears. When we free ourselves from *those* things, we shall be truly free, and so will the world.

But I am also reminded of the Civil Guard on the beach in Spain, rifle slung from his shoulder, clutching in his hand a small, blind rabbit. Time had run out for the rabbit and time is running out for us too, so it is vital that we open our eyes and see. Only when we can see shall we be able to shake ourselves free from the tyranny of material power. We were told on good authority that, "Ye shall know the truth and the truth shall make you free," and to know the truth is truly to see. Truly to see is, of course, to have vision, and vision is what we are looking for.

So what *is* the truth that makes us free? Some would say that it is the understanding of our oneness with God, but how many of us have any direct experience of oneness? On the other hand, love is something that we all know about—or think we do—and the truth that makes us free pertains in part to love. When human beings express love, they are in fact expressing God, because, as Christ revealed, the nature of God *is* love. Through love, therefore, God's presence manifests in the world; but, most importantly, when God's presence manifests in the world, the almighty power of God manifests too— hence the saying, "Love conquers all."

That may sound absurdly simple, and it is. Christ's two commandments were simple too. If obeyed, they would no doubt change the world, but by and large they are not obeyed, and for two reasons: the world is full of fear, and fear inhibits love. It is true that an understanding of the almighty power of God should banish fear and so make it possible to love, but who believes in the almighty power of God? Many pay lip-service to the concept, but few behave as though they really believe it. This is partly because God's power manifests in human affairs in proportion to our ability to love, and, since most of the time we fail to love, most people see little evidence for any such power. But unless God *is* almighty it would be absurd to claim that love conquers all, so the question, Is God really almighty?, demands an answer. Each must find that answer in his or her own way. I found it through art.

The other day I was wondering about the source of power in a work of art. Where does this power come from? Roger Fry said that "The essential power of pictorial as of all other arts lies in its use of a fundamental and universal symbolism." If I understand him correctly, Fry is implying that the source of power in a work of art is to be found in its content, or subject matter, but the fact remains that no work of art has stood the test of time by virtue of its content alone. In the case of certain works of art the significance of the subject, no doubt of prime importance to the artist, has been long forgotten, and yet these pieces still have the power to move us. Music, with obvious exceptions, is wholly abstract, and the same is true of much contemporary painting and sculpture; it *has* no subject matter and yet the power of such work is often undeniable. It is true that subject matter often appears to be the source of

79. "YE SHALL KNOW THE TRUTH"   66″ × 82″   1978

power, that it is often what moves us, or strikes a chord in the unconscious, but then again no subject matter, universal or otherwise, is going to carry much weight if it is feebly expressed. So the power of subject matter, being dependent on something other than itself, cannot itself be the *source* of power.

By this I do not mean to imply that subject matter is unimportant. Who would say that the subject of the Buddha, for instance, was unimportant to the sculptors of Elephanta, or the subject of the gospel unimportant to those who made the stained glass windows of Chartres? Clearly the subject was of enormous importance to these artists. Furthermore, their works remain of importance to countless thousands to this day. The artists in question were, of course, testifying to eternal truths, but is this the only reason why we are moved by such works? In fact, would we be moved by them at all if they were not consummate works of art? The answer would have to be that, in all likelihood, we would not.

So, however sublime the subject, whether or not we are moved by it is dependent on *how* it is depicted. Of course there will always be those who can see no further than the subject and, if they are moved at all, will presume that it is because of the subject. It is true that such people may admire the artist's skill in rendering the actual forms of nature, but as soon as the artist deviates from those actual forms they are lost. This is because they look at works of art as if they were meant to be literal descriptions of nature and fail to realize that art is a language all its own and one that requires no literal descriptions, or literary allusions, to elicit emotion. The true language of art is the language of aesthetics. Those who can understand this language have a ready-made stepping-stone to the Real World, for those who can see and appreciate the unity of a work of art are more likely to see and appreciate the unity of all things.*

The new physicists are certainly among those who see and appreciate the unity of all things. To quote from Fritjof Capra's The Turning Point *(p. 92): "... nature cannot be reduced to fundamental entities, like fundamental building blocks of matter, but has to be understood entirely through self-consistency. All of physics has to follow uniquely from the requirement that its components be consistent with one another and with themselves.... At the same time it is the culmination of the conception of the material world as an interconnected web of relations that emerged from quantum theory....The universe is seen as a dynamic web*

The language of aesthetics is a language of relationships—for instance, relationships of line, form and color constitute the language of painting—and we should look for the source of power in art in terms of its own language and not some other. One artist who spoke this language with unusual eloquence (without ever losing sight of subject matter) was Pablo Picasso. Though capable of depicting the actual forms of nature with the utmost fidelity, he is best known to the world at large as the great destroyer of natural forms, and it is true—he refused to make things easy for us. Instead, inspired by the work of Cezanne, he focused his relentless energy on spiritual truth,** testifying to the nature of oneness as few artists had ever done before, or been able to do since. For him, *that* was the point. Oneness was what mattered and all else was subjugated to that end. Picasso makes it easy for us to put our finger on the source of power in art because he forces us to look for it in terms of the language of art. His painting, *Guernica*, depicts the bombing of the small Spanish town of that name. It was the first deliberate bombing of civilians during the Spanish Civil War, and the painting stands as a timeless condemnation of all such acts of barbarism. It is a powerful painting, but not because of the horror of the subject matter—the painting itself is hardly horrific at all—but rather because of the stark contrast of the blacks and whites and the precise relationship of all the parts to the whole. It is powerful in terms of the language of art and not because of the subject. But the power is not in the parts—in the dark parts any more than in the light—but rather is it in the relationship *between* the parts. In other words, seeking in purely visual terms, the true source of power will be found in the *unity* of the work. And that is where the source of power is always

---

of interrelated events. None of the properties of any part of this web is fundamental; they all follow from the properties of the other parts, and the overall consistency of their interrelations determines the structure of the entire web." The same can be claimed for a work of art, for a work of art is entirely a question of interrelationships and is dependent on self-consistency too. In other words, what Capra is saying is that the universe itself is a work of art.

**Picasso's art is not usually thought of as spiritual—spirituality is normally associated with religion and Picasso was certainly not religious in a conventional sense—but Picasso's art is spiritual in terms of art, not religion. The point I am making is that art requires no religious connotations to be spiritual; art is its own "way of knowledge."

to be found in any work of art worthy of the name. Regardless of subject matter, or lack of subject matter, the power comes from the unified whole.

I have gone into this question at some length because I wanted to be sure of the answer. Within the context of the analogy that I sketched out in the previous chapter—and certainly from my own perspective as a painter—the answer is significant. In that chapter I suggested that the unified whole in art is analogous to the Real World, the Real World being simply another term for the Unified Whole we call "God." If the only true source of power in art is the unified whole, then to pursue the analogy to its logical conclusion, it follows that God is the only true source of power in life—that God is indeed *all*-mighty.*

I realize that for many this conclusion may be hard to accept, and for two reasons. The first is that there are so many things in the world that appear to be a source of power too; but such things are like content in a work of art which, though important to the viewer and essential to the artist, is not itself the source of power. Or they may be compared to the lights and darks in a painting, which are not the source of power either. But in practice we *do* ascribe power to the lights and darks—in other words, to all the myriad manifestations of good and evil in the world—never stopping to realize that there is only *one* source of power: God. It seems that not many of us know how to look at God—as few of us, in fact, as know how to look at paintings—and so we remain blind to the nature of God, blind to the real source of power. In other

---

*If God is the power of the Unified Whole, uniting both light and dark in a harmonious oneness, then it becomes quite clear why certain works of art are "transporting." If the artist or composer succeeds in bringing into "harmony or attunement" the tensions inherent in the composition, then the power generated thereby is the nearest many of us ever come to a glimpse, as it were, of God's face. On a more literal note, if we really want such a glimpse, all we have to do is listen to, say, a Bach concerto. The three-part format of much Baroque music is a wonderfully accurate portrayal of God, the first movement tending to the grand, the second to the lyrical and the third to the busy, thus suggesting the power of the Father, the love of the Son, and the activity of the Holy Spirit, all in exact relationship one to the other and all existing together in one unified whole. We are part of that whole—not separate from it. The second movement is our own Self-portrait.

words, we are like people who see no further than subject matter in art. Bewitched by the subject matter of the world—the "reality" we ourselves have made—we fail to understand the language of the Real World. We do not perceive the oneness, and hence fail to perceive the power.

The second reason why some people find it hard to accept the concept of an almighty God is because they see a world full of evil and suffering and think, How can God possibly be almighty if, as Christ led us to believe, God is a God of love? The usual answer to that question is that God gave us free will; but there is another answer—uncomfortable though it may be—that seems to me more to the point. The almighty power of God *is* a reality, but it is the reality of the Real World, not our world. Material power is our reality, our world being the world of "strife between opposites." This being so, we are cut off from the true safety and security of God's power. It should be born in mind that a work of art reflects the Real World, not our world, and that the power emanating from the unified whole only does so because the artist has *transcended* "the strife between opposites." But we have transcended no such thing, so if we would have access to the power of God, we have first to find a means of access to the Real World. This is not as impossible as it may sound. The creative process shows us the way. By obeying the rules of this process, artists achieve unity in their work, and by obeying the same rules we gain access to the Real World. In other words, by obeying Christ's two commandments—for the two commandments *are* the rules of the creative process—we gain access to the almighty power of God. Of course, God's power, or spiritual power, is not something we can use—it uses us.

But even if we know the truth that makes us free, it is often hard to remain true to one's vision. By this I mean that it is hard not to be fooled by appearances, for the evils of the world are so hideously real that most would think it tantamount to lunacy to say that they present no threat. They are indeed real, but only in terms of our "reality," and never in terms of God's Reality. If we would banish fear, we need to see *through* our "reality," and the best way of doing that is to understand what created it in the first place. When we see through our "reality" we see the Real World, for the Real World is here and now.

The Tibetan Buddhists understood our "reality" precisely and have given us an image to account for it. Mind, Speech, and Form, the Three Lords of Materialism, personify not only the mental processes that produce good and evil in the world, but the words that give form to the thoughts, and the three-dimensional forms that in turn are given form by thoughts and words. We love the good and fear the evil, and because we fear the evil we are vulnerable to it. All forms of evil emanate from a false sense of separation from God, but, since it is literally impossible to separate ourselves from God, it follows that all forms of evil emanate from a lie. Since the forms themselves are based on a lie, the power that we attribute to those forms must be a lie too. In other words, the Three Lords of Materialism are liars, their thoughts deluded, their words false, their forms nothing but bluff and bluster. Their power is maintained and sus-

80. THE ILLUSION OF THE GIANTS II   80″ × 64″   1980

tained by our belief in them, but the moment we see through them their power begins to crumble, our fear dissolves, and we are free.

But simply knowing what is *not* power leaves a vacuum. We also have to know what *is* power. Love is true power, but even that knowledge is not enough; we have to know *why* love is true power. As I have said before, love is true power because when we express love we express God. In other words, when we express love, God enters the human scene and, when God enters the human scene, the almighty power of God enters the human scene too. When that happens, all forms of human material power lose their dominance. So to the extent that we express love we are invincible; to the extent that we fail to love we are vulnerable.

As it is, the so-called "super-powers," by possessing an arsenal of deadly weapons, which is a flagrant denial of love, and by relying on that arsenal for their safety and security, have effectively cut themselves off from the true safety and security of the almighty power of God. Living under the wing of such a "super-power" is not a comfortable feeling. Furthermore, whenever we supply arms to other nations, or factions within nations, we separate ourselves still further from God. Do our leaders fail to realize what these weapons *do* to people? Traffic in arms is a form of terrorism—terrorism, the antithesis of love.

Nietzsche had the right idea when he said, "Rather perish than hate and fear, and twice rather perish than make oneself hated and feared." Love is implicit in Nietzsche's statement, and provided we know what to affirm about love, there is no need to perish. Love really does conquer all. Love cuts through opposing ideologies. It not only sees the other person simply as another human being whom we should care about—someone who may well hold different opinions, but with joys and sorrows and needs like ourselves—but it sees the Kingdom within every man, woman and child on the face of the Earth. Love ignores appearances; it sees the Christ in all human beings, even our enemies. That recognition is praying for our enemies, and there is much power in such prayer. But love must be expressed in action as well, so before taking action nations would do well to stop and ask themselves, Is the action in question an expression of love? This simple yardstick would work miracles, for by taking action based on love we would be opening the way for God's power to manifest in the world. It is then God's presence—and not ourselves—that would resolve the outcome. When that happens, of certain things we may be sure—where there was disorder there would be order; where there was strife, harmony; where there was lack, plenty; where there was suffering, joy; for such is the nature of God's grace.

We are all children of God, but if we are to claim our inheritance, which is the Real World, we have to know *how* to love. Love is a question of focus. Just as the success or failure of a painting is dependent on the artist's ability to see the part within the context of the whole and to love both, so the success or failure of the human race is dependent on our ability to see and love the world as a whole and each and every part within it. The broader our perspective, the closer we come to loving God; the greater our attention to detail, the closer we come to loving our neighbor.

Artists know from continual experience that this dual focus works and, furthermore, that it is the only sort of focus that does work. They rely on this focus every time they put brush to canvas, and know that without it they are lost. Similarly, Christ's two commandments are not a question of ethics, they are pure pragmatism: if we want to solve our problems, this is what we have to do. If we fail to follow Christ's advice we are all lost; but, even though we have failed consistently for two thousand years, there is still time to act on it. Perhaps circumstances are finally forcing us to act on it. But, forced or not, a choice has to be made, and only we can make it. It is a simple choice: we can fail to love, and perish, or we can learn to love, and live—for the rules of the creative process are not to be denied. Love is the universal imperative.

81. ALL THE PEOPLE SEE THE LIGHT   82″ × 66″   1971

NOTES

1. P.D. Ouspensky, A New Model of the Universe *(London: Routledge and Kegan Paul, Ltd., 1960), 35.*

2. Elaine Pagels, The Gnostic Gospels *(Vintage Books, 1981), 172.*

3. Pagels, The Gnostic Gospels, *172.*

4. Robert Graves, The White Goddess *(Farrar, Straus & Giroux, 1966), 368.*

5. Chogyam Trungpa, Cutting Through Spiritual Materialism *(Shambhala, 1973), 5.*

6. C.G. Jung, Flying Saucers: A Modern Myth of Things Seen in the Skies, *Bollingen Series (Princeton University Press, 1978), 21.*

7. Graves, The White Goddess, *394.*

8. Monica Furlong, Merton: A Biography *(Harper & Row, 1980), 231.*

9. Pauline Matarasso, The Quest of the Holy Grail *(Penguin Books, 1969).*

10. Heinrich Zimmer, The King and the Corpse, *Bollingen Series XI (Princeton University Press, 1948), 34.*

11. Roger Fry, Vision and Design *(Pelican Books, 1937), 180.*

12. Ibid., *244.*

13. Ouspensky, A New Model of the Universe, *34.*

14. Ibid., *35.*

15. Bertrand Russell, Wisdom of the West *(Crescent Books, Inc., 1959), 24.*

16. Graves, The White Goddess, *476.*

LIST OF ILLUSTRATIONS

TITLE	DATE	SIZE	MEDIUM	OWNER
Cover: RIVER CROSSING I	1974	47″ × 33″	acrylic on canvas	Mr. & Mrs. John Karr, Texas
1. THE HERMIT	1978	25″ × 24″	India ink & acrylic on board	Mr. & Mrs. Will Channing, Massachusetts
2. THE PROPOSAL	1979	82″ × 60″	acrylic & oil on canvas	Mr. & Mrs. Robert Enfield, New Mexico
3. THE ENTRANCE TO THE FOREST I	1974	14″ × 13″	India ink & acrylic on wood	Eastern New Mexico University, Roswell
4a. THE GIFT II	1975	16″ × 12″	India ink on gesso	Mr. Paul Coupey, New Mexico
4b. MAN, WOMAN, HORSE, AND DOVE	1974	12″ × 10″	India ink & acrylic on wood	Eastern New Mexico University, Roswell

PART ONE, CHAPTER ONE

TITLE	DATE	SIZE	MEDIUM	OWNER
5. MAN CROSSING A BRIDGE	1949	7″ × 12″ approx.	pen & ink	Mr. & Mrs. P. N. Rogers, U.K.
6. THE CRUCIFIXION	1957	70″ × 120″ approx.	oil on board	Mr. & Mrs. Alistair McAlpine, U.K.
7. WAVING WOMAN	1959	10″ × 36″	oil on board	Mr. & Mrs. Graham Burge, U.K.
8. TWO STANDING WOMEN	1959	14″ × 15″	oil on board	M.V.B. Hill. Esq., U.K.
9. THREE STANDING WOMEN	1959	13″ × 14″	oil on board	M.V.B. Hill, Esq., U.K.
10. AN IMAGE OF EVIL	1959	30″ × 40″	oil on canvas	Mr. & Mrs. John Diehl, New Mexico
11. THE ILLUSION OF SEPARATENESS	1960	36″ × 48″	oil on board	Mr. & Mrs. David Wynne, U.K.
12. THE UNDERSTANDING OF ONENESS	1960	36″ × 48″	oil on board	Mr. & Mrs. David Wynne, U.K.
13. THE GIANTS I	1972	12″ × 11″	India ink & acrylic on wood	Mr. & Mrs. Allan Ely, Texas
14. THE ILLUSION OF THE GIANTS I	1975	16″ × 12″	acrylic on wood	Mr. & Mrs. Robert Enfield, New Mexico
15. THE THREE LORDS OF MATERIALISM I	1980	64″ × 80″	oil on canvas	Mr. & Mrs. Robert Wagschal, Holland
16. THE THREE MUSES	1980	68″ × 80″	oil on canvas	Mr. & Mrs. Tom O'Connor, New Mexico
17. NEW PARADIGM I	1983	120″ × 102″	oil on canvas	Ms. Maria Anderson Sardy, Alaska
18. NEW PARADIGM II	1986	42″ × 40″	oil on canvas	The Rev. & Mrs. Roy Cole, New Mexico

CHAPTER TWO

TITLE	DATE	SIZE	MEDIUM	OWNER
19. FALLEN BRANCH	1969	18″ × 12″	pen and wash	Mr. David McIntosh, New Mexico

CHAPTER THREE

20. THE HERALD	1979	82″ × 66″	oil on canvas	Mr. & Mrs. Don Calvin, New Mexico
21. AN ANNUNCIATION	1960	48″ × 72″	oil on board	Lady Crathorne, U.K.
22. CHRIST WALKING ON THE WATER	1960	31″ × 25″	oil on canvas	Miss Margaret Davies, U.K.
23. GETHSEMANE	1960	36″ × 28″	oil on canvas	Mr. & Mrs. P.A. Hamblen, U.K.
24. CRUCIFIXION TRIPTYCH	1960	60″ × 31″	oil on canvas	Mr. & Mrs. Robin Huntington, U.K.
25. CHRIST SHOWING HIS WOUNDS	1960	32″ × 24″	oil on canvas	Miss Ruth Murell, U.K.
26. THE DESCENT FROM THE CROSS	1960	31″ × 25″	oil on canvas	Mrs. J.J. Evans, U.K.
27. MARTHA AND MARY	1961	30″ × 28″	oil on canvas	Mr. & Mrs. Whitaker, U.K.
28. THE MONEYCHANGERS	1961	36″ × 28″	oil on canvas	F.A. Gray, Esq., U.K.
29. THE RESURRECTION	1961	40″ × 30″	oil on canvas	R.R. Voeleker, Esq., U.K.
30. WASHING THE APOSTLES' FEET	1961	20″ × 12″	oil on canvas	M.V.B. Hill, Esq., U.K.
31. THE ASCENSION I	1962	36″ × 25″	acrylic & oil on canvas	The artist
32. THE ASCENSION II	1962	40″ × 50″	oil on canvas	Mrs. Robin McCoy Bent, New Hampshire
33. THE ASCENSION III	1962	45″ × 60″	oil on canvas	Douglas Cochrane, Esq., U.K.
34. THE ASCENSION IV	1963	24″ × 10″	pen & wash collage	Miss Thetis Blacker, U.K.
35. THE COMET III	1983	8″ × 6″	acrylic on wood	Mr. & Mrs. Bill Martin, New Mexico
36. THE BIRTH OF VENUS	1967	72″ × 48″	oil on board	The artist
37. HEAD OF A GIRL	1972	14″ × 16″	oil on wood	Mrs. Dan Griffith, New Mexico
38. THE RETURN OF THE DOVE I	1978	76″ × 66″	acrylic on canvas	Mr. Michael Zakroff, New Mexico
39. THE MARRIAGE OF HEAVEN AND EARTH	1981	72″ × 68″	oil on canvas	Mr. Richard Gooding, Colorado
40. THE NATIVITY	1961	40″ × 50″	oil on canvas	The artist

CHAPTER FOUR

41. SAINT IN MEDITATION	1960	52″ × 60″	oil on board	Mr. & Mrs. Spencer Teakle, Spain
42. A VISION OF THE VIRGIN AND CHILD	1972	10″ × 9″	India ink & acrylic on wood	Mr. & Mrs. Ted Robertson, New Mexico
43. HERMIT PEELING AN APPLE	1972	10″ × 9″	India ink & acrylic on wood	Miss Thetis Blacker, U.K.
44. THE TEACHER	1975	11″ × 11″	acrylic on wood	Mr. & Mrs. Harold Carter, Colorado
45. HERMIT WITH SHEEP	1972	9″ × 10″	India ink & acrylic on wood	Mr. Walter Limacher, New Mexico
46. HERMIT WITH CAT AND BIRD	1972	40″ × 29″	India ink & acrylic on wood	Mr. & Mrs. Robert Enfield, New Mexico

THE QUEST

I. THE GIANTS II	1974	19″ × 17″	India ink & acrylic on canvas	Ms. Tish Gallenkamp, New Mexico
II. THE CRUSADERS III	1974	17″ × 19″	India ink & acrylic on canvas	Mr. & Mrs. Harold Carter, Colorado
III. THE CRUSADERS IV	1974	15″ × 18″	India ink & acrylic on canvas	Mr. & Mrs. Bill Smith, New Mexico
IV. THE CRUSADERS I	1973	16″ × 11″	India ink & acrylic on canvas	Mrs. Elizabeth Stevenson, California
V. THE CRUSADERS II	1973	16″ × 18″	India ink & acrylic on canvas	Mr. Eugene Nearburg, Texas
VI. FLIGHT	1974	12″ × 10″	India ink & acrylic on wood	Eastern New Mexico University, Roswell
VII. THE GIFT I	1975	19″ × 16″	acrylic on wood	Mr. & Mrs. Abel Davis, New Mexico
VIII. THE ABYSS	1974	12″ × 16″	India ink & acrylic on wood	Eastern New Mexico University, Roswell
IX. THE SECOND MUSE (MEMORY)	1972	83″ × 66″	India ink & acrylic on canvas	Mr. & Mrs. Robert O. Anderson, New Mexico
X. THE DOVE	1972	86″ × 68″	India ink & acrylic on canvas	Mr. & Mrs. Robert Brunn, New Mexico
XI. THE CHANNEL	1972	67″ × 101″	India ink & acrylic on canvas	Mr. Eugene Nearburg, Texas
XII. BYSTANDERS	1975	12″ × 11″	acrylic on wood	Mr. Tug Wilson, New Mexico
XIII. THE MOUNTAINTOP	1974	17″ × 19″	India ink & acrylic on canvas	Mr. & Mrs. Barry Rusler, New Mexico
XIV. THE WAY	1985	18″ × 16″	oil on canvas	Mr. & Mrs. P.N. Rogers, U.K.
XV. THE ENTRANCE TO THE FOREST II	1975	16″ × 12″	acrylic on board	Mr. & Mrs. George Limacher, New Mexico
XVI. FOREST PATHS	1975	11″ × 15″	acrylic on wood	Mr. & Mrs. Keith Yarborough, New Mexico
XVII. FALL	1980	56″ × 80″	oil on canvas	Mr. & Mrs. Neil Jampolis, New York
XVIII. THE STORM	1975	16″ × 12″	India ink & acrylic on board	Mr. & Mrs. Don Graves, California
XIX. THE RETURN OF THE DOVE II	1975	17″ × 14″	acrylic on wood	Mr. Eugene Nearburg, Texas
XX. GIFTS	1985	84″ × 48″	oil on canvas	Mr. & Mrs. Jim Eldridge, Colorado
XXI. THE COMET II	1978	10″ × 10″	acrylic on canvas	Ms. Debra Incendio, New Mexico
XXII. THE POOL II	1978	50″ × 43″	acrylic on canvas	ARCO Collection
XXIII. SUNRISE III	1980	66″ × 70″	oil on canvas	Mrs. Marion Bumpass, Texas
XXIV. METAMORPHOSIS	1980	82″ × 66″	oil on canvas	Mr. & Mrs. Don Calvin, New Mexico
XXV. THE SECOND BAPTISM II	1982	60″ × 78″	oil on canvas	Mrs. Peter Hurd, New Mexico
XXVI. ASCENSION	1975	12″ × 14″	India ink & acrylic on board	Mr. Jeremy Chisholm, New Mexico

CHAPTER FIVE

47.	HEADGATE, detail of mural	1974	16′ × 10′ (40′ × 17′)	India ink on gesso	Texas Tech University Museum, Lubbock
48.	HERMIT AND HEADGATE	1975	17″ × 14″	India ink & acrylic on wood	Mr. & Mrs. Chet Olsen, New Mexico
49.	THE RIVER	1975	86″ × 48″	India ink & acrylic on canvas	Mr. Eugene Nearburg, Texas

CHAPTER SIX

50.	THE FLIGHT INTO EGYPT	1972	9″ × 9″	India ink & acrylic on wood	Mrs. Helen O'Leary, Florida
51.	THE SECOND BAPTISM I	1982	66″ × 80″	acrylic & oil on canvas	Mr. & Mrs. Israel Miranda, New Mexico
52.	CATACLYSM I	1975	11″ × 15″	pencil & acrylic on wood	Mr. Tug Wilson, New Mexico
53.	TRIAL BY WATER	1985	25″ × 16″	acrylic & oil on wood	Mr. & Mrs. Jim Eldridge, Colorado
54.	TRIAL BY FIRE	1985	25″ × 16″	acrylic & oil on wood	Mr. & Mrs. Jim Eldridge, Colorado
55.	THE FOOL	1971	19″ × 16″	pencil on gesso	Mrs. Goddard Lieberson, New York

PART TWO, CHAPTER SEVEN

56.	SUNRISE I	1974	13″ × 10″	pen & ink and acrylic on wood	Eastern New Mexico University, Roswell
57.	CARDPLAYERS	1956	40″ × 30″ approx.	oil on board	Mrs. O.D. Paget-Cooke, U.K.
58.	PORTRAIT OF JENNY	1958	19″ × 24″	oil on canvas	Mrs. Beth Huntington, U.K.
59.	SELF-PORTRAIT	1959	12″ × 14″	oil on board	Mr. & Mrs. James Parrish, U.K.
60.	PORTRAIT OF DEBORAH	1963	8″ × 12″	pencil on paper	Mr. & Mrs. Emmanuel Kaye, U.K.
61.	FEMALE NUDE	1955		pencil on paper	owner unknown
62.	MALE NUDE I	1955		conté crayon	Mr. & Mrs. Robert V. Ely, New Mexico
63.	MALE NUDE II	1955		conté crayon	owner unknown
64.	PORTRAIT OF GILLIAN	1979	20″ × 25″ approx.	pen & ink and acrylic on canvas	Mr. & Mrs. David Wynne, U.K.
65.	RIO HONDO	1964	18″ × 24″ approx.	pen & wash on paper	Mr. & Mrs. Robert O. Anderson, New Mexico
66.	ARROYO	1964	24″ × 18″ approx.	pen & wash on paper	Mr. & Mrs. Robert O. Anderson, New Mexico
67.	RANCH ROAD	1964	30″ × 21″	pen & wash on paper	Mr. & Mrs. Robert O. Anderson, New Mexico
68.	PORTRAIT OF JAMES	1956	30″ × 48″	oil on board	Mr. & Mrs. James Parrish, U.K.
69.	DRILLING RIG, PRUDHOE BAY	1969	30″ × 22″	pen & wash	ARCO Collection
70.	DRAWWORKS AND SWIVEL	1969	30″ × 22″	pen & wash	ARCO Collection
71.	"CHRISTMAS TREE"	1969	22″ × 30″	pen & wash	ARCO Collection
72.	HERMIT PAINTING A BIRD	1975	19″ × 16″	pen & ink and acrylic on canvas	Mr. & Mrs. Robert O. Anderson, New Mexico

LIST OF ILLUSTRATIONS

CHAPTER EIGHT

ABOUT THE AUTHOR

Peter Rogers was born in London on August 24, 1933. There were no other painters in his family, although his maternal grandfather, Harry Marillier, was closely associated with the Pre-Raphaelites and was the leading authority of his day on tapestry. Rogers was educated at Sherborne. After doing his National Service (basic training in the Welsh Guards, 2nd lieutenant in the Queen's Royal Regiment) he studied at St. Martin's School of Art in London. In 1957 he was elected a member of the Royal Society of British Artists, and in 1960 Arthur Tooth and Sons became his exclusive dealer in London. In 1962 he went to live in Spain and, while there, met Carol Hurd, daughter of the painters, Peter Hurd and Henriette Wyeth Hurd. Having moved to the United States in 1963, he and Carol were married and took up residence on the Hurd's ranch at San Patricio, New Mexico. Since then, Rogers' painting has alternated between a variety of commissioned work and the development of the Quest theme, the latter having been his predominant and abiding interest. After a sojourn in Santa Fe from 1975-83, the Rogers returned to San Patricio, where they continue to live and work. They have three children, Peter, Gabriela, and David, the last of whom is also a painter.